MARKETING AND OPERATIONS MANAGEMENT RESEARCH

MARKETING RESEARCH FOR SMALL BUSINESS

AN EFFICIENT AND EFFECTIVE FUNCTIONAL APPROACH

MARKETING AND OPERATIONS MANAGEMENT RESEARCH

Additional books and e-books in this series can be found on Nova's website under the Series tab.

MARKETING AND OPERATIONS MANAGEMENT RESEARCH

MARKETING RESEARCH FOR SMALL BUSINESS

AN EFFICIENT AND EFFECTIVE FUNCTIONAL APPROACH

DAVID J. SMITH
AND
BARBARA A. VANDERWERF

Copyright © 2018 by Nova Science Publishers, Inc.

All rights reserved. No part of this book may be reproduced, stored in a retrieval system or transmitted in any form or by any means: electronic, electrostatic, magnetic, tape, mechanical photocopying, recording or otherwise without the written permission of the Publisher.

We have partnered with Copyright Clearance Center to make it easy for you to obtain permissions to reuse content from this publication. Simply navigate to this publication's page on Nova's website and locate the "Get Permission" button below the title description. This button is linked directly to the title's permission page on copyright.com. Alternatively, you can visit copyright.com and search by title, ISBN, or ISSN.

For further questions about using the service on copyright.com, please contact:
Copyright Clearance Center
Phone: +1-(978) 750-8400   Fax: +1-(978) 750-4470   E-mail: info@copyright.com.

NOTICE TO THE READER

The Publisher has taken reasonable care in the preparation of this book, but makes no expressed or implied warranty of any kind and assumes no responsibility for any errors or omissions. No liability is assumed for incidental or consequential damages in connection with or arising out of information contained in this book. The Publisher shall not be liable for any special, consequential, or exemplary damages resulting, in whole or in part, from the readers' use of, or reliance upon, this material. Any parts of this book based on government reports are so indicated and copyright is claimed for those parts to the extent applicable to compilations of such works.

Independent verification should be sought for any data, advice or recommendations contained in this book. In addition, no responsibility is assumed by the publisher for any injury and/or damage to persons or property arising from any methods, products, instructions, ideas or otherwise contained in this publication.

This publication is designed to provide accurate and authoritative information with regard to the subject matter covered herein. It is sold with the clear understanding that the Publisher is not engaged in rendering legal or any other professional services. If legal or any other expert assistance is required, the services of a competent person should be sought. FROM A DECLARATION OF PARTICIPANTS JOINTLY ADOPTED BY A COMMITTEE OF THE AMERICAN BAR ASSOCIATION AND A COMMITTEE OF PUBLISHERS.

Additional color graphics may be available in the e-book version of this book.

Library of Congress Cataloging-in-Publication Data

Names: Smith, David J. (Professor of management), author. | VanderWerf, Barbara A., author.
Title: Marketing research for small business: an efficient and effective functional approach / David J. Smith and Barbara A. VanderWerf (Faculty, Rinker School of Business, Palm Beach Atlantic University, West Palm Beach, FL).
Description: Hauppauge, New York: Nova Science Publishers, Inc., [2018] | Series: Marketing and operations management research | Includes index.
Identifiers: LCCN 2018037646 (print) | LCCN 2018040117 (ebook) | ISBN 9781536140446 (ebook) | ISBN 9781536140422 (hardcover)
Subjects: LCSH: Marketing research. | Small business. | Small business marketing.
Classification: LCC HF5415.2 (ebook) | LCC HF5415.2 .S563 2018 (print) | DDC 658.8/3--dc23
LC record available at https://lccn.loc.gov/2018037646

Published by Nova Science Publishers, Inc. † New York

Contents

List of Figures		vii
Preface		ix
Acknowledgments		xi
Chapter 1	Why Marketing Research?	1
Chapter 2	Common Misunderstandings	11
Chapter 3	The Research Agenda	23
Chapter 4	Using the Functional Approach	37
Chapter 5	Working First with What You Have	57
Chapter 6	Collecting Information	73
Chapter 7	Basic Surveys	89
Chapter 8	Leveraging Social Media	117
Chapter 9	Working with Results	131
Chapter 10	Statistics Primer	147
Chapter 11	Making It Count	173
Appendix 1.	Online Resources	189

Appendix 2.	Sample Surveys	**199**
Appendix 3.	Top Global Marketing Research Firms	**213**
About the Authors		**217**
Index		**219**

LIST OF FIGURES

Figure 3.1.	A Common Research Planning Approach.	24
Figure 3.2.	Research Planning Resource Potential.	25
Figure 4.1.	Traditional Research Approach.	48
Figure 4.2.	A Functional Approach to Marketing Research.	49
Figure 10.1.	Numerical Categories for Statistical Analysis.	150
Figure 10.2.	Central Tendency Observation.	152
Figure 10.3.	Distribution Curve Examples.	154
Figure 10.4.	Variant Regression Lines.	166

PREFACE

The impacts of small business on our economy continue to be significant as both job growth and revenues are expanding. Small business owners and entrepreneurs continue to look for ways to breakout their product offerings and one of the most common conduits for that is through aggressive marketing. Most small business owners agree that promoting their products effectively leads to increased customer activity which leads to increased sales. Here is the problem, most of these owners and entrepreneurs do not know much about marketing and are often unsure about how to proceed. They have a general idea about advertising and promotion but fall short especially when it comes to gathering intelligent useful marketing information. There is a perceived complexity and high cost surrounding marketing research so it often becomes ignored. This misstep results in inefficient and ineffective marketing efforts, further resulting in miscommunication with the customer and unrealized sales.

Marketing research not only serves as the underpinning for all advertising efforts, but commonly identifies areas of new opportunities business owners did not even recognize existed. Using this simplified cost effective functional approach will allow owners to engage in simple, useful and impactful information gathering. This will serve as the backbone for all of their future marketing efforts. This book provides a step by step approach to conduct marketing research that will not be expensive or confusing. It also provides real examples that make sense. The ultimate goal of this book is to provide small business owners and entrepreneurs with confidence in their understanding of marketing research and the tools necessary to begin increasing their sales.

Acknowledgments

To all of those who have influenced us and inspired us throughout our management experience, thank you.

Helping others succeed is one of our chief commitments. Part of our responsibility as professors is to equip students with the tools to learn, grow, and succeed in business. Their success inspires us to share more.

For this reason, we dedicate this book to small business owners like us who have the desire to learn, grow, and succeed! We trust this book will provide valuable, practical, on-the-ground ideas for efficient and effective marketing research and by applying these methods in your firm you will see an increase in organizational performance!

Chapter 1

WHY MARKETING RESEARCH?

The fact that you picked up this book would suggest one of two things. Either you are familiar with marketing research and are curious if there are any easy tips to pick up regarding your marketing program, or you have little to no understanding of marketing research and would like to learn more. In either case, you should be commended for your willingness to keep learning.

There are many complexities to marketing and most business people will tell you this is an area of business they know a lot about. This is rarely the case. While selling and advertising are certainly components of marketing, there is still much more to the process. In particular, one area where most firms underperform is in marketing research. Chapter Two will provide some insight as to why, but for now, we can focus on the importance of marketing research.

Most marketers agree that market research is critical - this is because the competitive landscape is always changing. This, coupled with changing company objectives and resources, creates a very fluid environment. Having knowledge and insight into this environment leads to opportunities which often turn into revenues. Furthermore, it limits the guesswork of decision-making, eliminating inefficiency, and eradicating ineffectiveness. Especially with small firms, they do not have the ability to absorb costly decision mistakes such as improper product positioning, low yield customer advertising and promotion, and poor targeting. For this reason, most fundamental marketing decisions should start with market and customer backed research.

In the broad sense, here are the common uses of marketing research.

The Small Business Administration defines small businesses based on either employee size or revenues. The pure definition is really not that important here and is primarily referred to throughout the book to suggest firms that do not have the wherewithal to consistently pay for or carry out research. Here are some parameters.

- Manufacturing: Maximum number of employees may range from 500 to 1500
- Wholesaling: Maximum number of employees may range from 100 to 500
- Services: Annual receipts may not exceed $2.5 to $21.5 million
- Retailing: Annual receipts may not exceed $5.0 to $21.0 million
- General and Heavy Construction: Annual receipts may not exceed $13.5 to $17 million
- Special Trade Construction: Annual receipts may not exceed $7 million

GENERAL BENEFITS OF MARKETING RESEARCH

Firms will not typically practice business activities unless there is some distinct or implied benefit. One of the early arguments for smaller firms is that marketing research does not provide clear, actionable benefit for the firm. If you only gain one thing from this book, it should be that marketing research provides enormous benefit to companies, regardless of size or scope. Specifically, here are four:

Voice of the Customer

To fully understand your customers' wants and needs, you have to formally ask them. This is the backbone of marketing research. Assuming wants and needs of customers is dangerous and usually inefficient. Communication methods are simple and can provide incredible depth into your customer.

Management Metrics

Managers are continuously making decisions within their firm. Decisions are the essence of the management function. A decision is nothing more than an assimilation of facts, an evaluation of facts, and a directed action on those facts. Notice that "facts" are the keys to decision-making. Marketing research generates facts! The more relevant facts you have, the easier the decision.

New Product

One inherent result of marketing research is the identification of new opportunities, often in the form of new products. Having an ability to look at the markets and identify trends and patterns can lead to new ideas and products for your business. You can get first-hand knowledge about what consumers want, and then act on that. Also, you can gain insight into current product feature shortcomings, and then correct, moving ahead of the competition.

Branding

Branding is the silent asset that underpins everything the firm does. Developing a brand that represents the reality of your firm and your products is a necessity for a competitive climate. Branding reinforces who you are, what you do, and how you do it. Marketing research allows firms to assess their current brand performance and adjust accordingly. What is the value of your brand? What do consumers think of your brand? And, what opportunities does branding allow for the future of my business? These are just a few branding questions answered by marketing research.

COMMON USES OF MARKETING RESEARCH

Market Intelligence

The common U.S. approach to marketing is a four-step process often taught in general marketing courses. The reason for its popularity is the efficient nature for acquiring new customers. The rationale is that it is focused on minimizing the cost to gain these new customers. Simply stated, "advertisement is more narrowly directed to customers more likely to buy your product."

1. *Identify* the overall market. How many people buy this product?
2. *Divide* the market into segments based on commonality, such as household income, age, zip code, or ethnic group.
3. *Target* specific segments most likely to purchase your product.
4. *Advertise* to those segments using media they would most likely use.

You can see from this process, there is a great deal of information needed to start the marketing process. Specific factors such as market size, in both number of customers and dollars, variables associated with market segmentation, identification and usage of different media outlets, and who currently sells in this market are just a few examples that require marketing research.

Existing Customers Behaviors

Understanding your current customers is critical to success. Not only does this allow your insight as to who your customers are, it also gives you a more well-defined direction for reaching new customers. For example, if 90 percent of your customers are between the ages of 20 and 30, it would probably be most advantageous to seek new customers in the same age bracket. Marketing is sometimes more about duplication than invention. The manager will want to consider the following general customer research areas:

- Why do customers select your products or those of your competitors?
- What factors influence buying decisions?
- Who are your customers?
- When do they shop?
- What value do they perceive in your products?
- What is the key decision factor for purchase?
- How do they find you?

More specific questions might be ...

- What product attributes are positive and negative?
- Are there new potential products to offer?
- Did customers ever buy from competitors?
- How old are your customers?
- Where to they live?
- What are their hobbies?
- How important is price to their purchase?

Competitor Analysis

Market research can also uncover variety of market variables and intelligence. You do not compete in a vacuum. For every customer you are trying to get or keep, another competing company is also trying to get or keep those same customers. It is imperative to understand who these other firms are and what they are doing (or planning to do) to get "your" customers. Some of these variables might be about price, similar and different attributes of their product, promotional offerings and approaches, distribution outlets such as online or on ground. In essence, you want to know the best way to keep your customers away from your competitors. No different than in any other competition, your firm will probably prevail if it knows more about the competitor than they know about you and you can exploit this knowledge to your benefit. This comes from marketing research!

New Business Opportunities

One common purpose for market research is to identify new business opportunities. These opportunities can come in various forms such as new products, new outlets for distribution, new customer segments, or new advertisement options. In a quest for increased sales, any or all of these may be the answer. A couple of specific approaches are through product perceptual mapping and multi-attribute gapping. These approaches are marketing tools, supported by market research that identify underserved areas of the market and underserved features of the product. These and other similar tools lead to an ability to meet the needs of the current and potential customer first.

Ongoing Business Decision-Making

Sometimes firms just need to make some business decisions. These decisions are either unique or repetitive. No matter the type, marketing research can often assist with the decision. Bounded rationality suggests that all decisions are made without perfect information - however, management gurus will tell you that the more information you have, the better the decision outcome will be (as long as it is relevant information). Normally, decisions illicit some characteristic of risk and return. Should we buy this or that? Should we open a new location here or there? Should be change the price or not? Should we advertise more or less? This set of common decisions call all be supported by increased marketing intelligence.

Many years ago, firms operated with the notion that no matter the product, if we utilized a selling orientation, we could sell anything, focusing on the transaction itself. This is no longer the case. Buyers are much more sophisticated and informed. We are now in a marketing orientation era. This suggests that before we even make the product, we need to know who will buy it and at what price. The contention here is that ALL firm decision making involving revenues can be supported by additional marketing research.

Lastly, decision making may require future predictions. Predictions require data and date comes from research. The collection of data does not need to be sophisticated - you may need to just track activity. This is particularly important with budgeting and resource allocation. In predicting future activity, firms can support and maintain appropriate levels of resource use. Too much or too little would be inefficient.

What about the Startup?

Most of the discussion so far has been regarding the use of data and research for existing firms. Equally, if not more important, is the marketing research potential firms perform before opening. As noted above, certain levels of understanding and confidence are required when estimating markets and future returns. Budding entrepreneurs and investors also need to make risk and return decisions based on expected outcomes. Is the market big enough? Is our product in demand? What are the features potential customers want? Is the pricing structure feasible? These are just a few questions that need answering before anything moves forward.

Most business plan templates have a section on breakeven analysis. The breakeven point represents what is required to cover total costs (both fixed and variable) and at the breakeven point, profit is zero.

Breakeven Point

$$\text{Fixed Costs} / \text{Unit Selling Price} - \text{Variable Unit Cost} = \text{Breakeven}$$

The ability to calculate a breakeven cannot even be considered unless certain assumptions are made. These assumptions should be made on an accurate reflection of reality, which comes from marketing research.

For example:

Fixed Costs per month: $5,000
Unit Selling Price: $4
Variable Unit Cost $1.50

The equation would be: $5000/$2.50 = 2000 units per month.

If you want to look per day, divide fixed costs by number of days open. ($5000/20 days)/$2.50 = 100 units per day

If you are open 8 hours a day, your hourly BE is 12.5 units.

Consider: Does current or future traffic support this level of sales?

Usually observations and counting will be sufficient at this point. Meaning, the potential firm could simply count movement and traffic patterns to get an idea about revenue viability. As simple as this sounds, it is still research. If your breakeven needs 20 customers an hour to purchase your product and only 30 drive by, it is likely your product in that location will not succeed. There is no need to start the business in that location and waste resources.

There are many online databases that can support some of this decision-making. Normally at any public library you can find several government and proprietary tools to help in your assessment of viability. This process is common sense. You have removed the emotional aspect of the decision and eliminated chance.

OUTPUT STAGES OF ANALYSIS

When looking at the research process from a holistic viewpoint, there are three primary macro tasks in marketing research. These encompass the three common perspectives: past-present-future. The common approach builds confidence and momentum in the process and normally generates additional research opportunities.

1. *Historical Report Review:* By reviewing historical data, you begin to build the perspective of both previous success and failure. Data will support and assist in explaining why particular initiatives did well or not. This allows the researcher a benchmark or starting point for research analysis. Also, at this point, definitions of success and failure become clearer to the firm.
2. *Analysis of Market and Customer:* As mentioned earlier in the chapter, this is what most business owners think of when contemplating market research. Data collected at this point certainly supports the tactical decisions such as target marketing, positioning, pricing, and media engagement. Gathering data regarding markets and customers underpins the owner's decisions

fundamental to selling and promotion. Furthermore, patterns of activity can be adjusted to reflect the reality of what is *really* happening versus what the owner *thinks* is happening.
3. *Prediction:* Another common outcome of market research is forecasting and prediction. Sometimes this can be a more daunting task because of the statistical nature of prediction, however it can be extremely useful. Being able to forecast and predict future activity, the firm can become more efficient, effective, and proactive. Small business owners are often put in difficult situations because of unforeseen events, leaving the owners playing catch up, feeling behind. Being ahead of or out in front of activity allows the owner to plan better and spend less.

Now you have a general idea of where we are headed in this book. The expectation after reading this is not to make you a research expert, but rather to increase your comfort level and confidence in undertaking a marketing research campaign and ultimately turning that research into revenue. A worst-case scenario is that you hire a marketing research firm and have them undertake the research. With this, you will have the tools to better understand their process, language, and results.

"An investment in knowledge pays the best interest."
Benjamin Franklin

Chapter 2

COMMON MISUNDERSTANDINGS

The most successful marketers are, without a doubt, those marketers armed with the most knowledge. They understand their markets, segments, targets, and the proper position of their products in relation to their audience. They also know which marketing tactics work and which ones do not. They instinctively recognize what their competition is doing almost as soon as they do it. Most importantly, successful marketers are acutely aware of what they do not know and are driven to learn and develop that knowledge base; once new information has been acquired, they are then able to use it in the most effective way.

Many business managers automatically understand this concept. They continually strive for more knowledge, specifically about their market position, realizing that better information leads to better competitive posturing. While managers of large businesses and corporations have the wherewithal to access many types of information services and are supported by a healthy budget, small and medium-sized organizations, from business sectors to nonprofit entities, do not usually have the level of resources available. They often come to one of the following conclusions:

- Even if we did have the money for research, we do not have the expertise and manpower to properly collect and interpret the information;
- We know marketing research is important, but we just don't have the budget;
- The cost-benefit does not seem to be there and we would probably be wasting our time on an effort that would not lead to significantly more sales;
- We do not know where to begin - it seems in a perfect world we could hire someone, but even then, would they be researching what we needed or would we be able to understand their results;
- We are not sure if we could tell the difference between good and bad research.

Negative thoughts regarding market research keep many managers from testing the proverbial research waters. These misunderstandings often flow directly from the marketing research arena, which has created a cloud of confusion and mystery around the subject of research. Marketing researchers have their own language and often have an air of superiority which implies that only those who are properly trained, "the research elite," are capable of conducting valid and reliable marketing research. This attitude, coupled with veneration for accepted research procedures and methods for how research should be conducted, created a daunting inner circle that many are fearful to break into. This is unfortunate since it keeps otherwise successful and proactive managers from considering marketing research as a viable option for improving, growing, and enhancing their business.

Understand that there are indeed situations when research professionals should be the prime sources for gathering and interpreting facts and data. There are also times when an impeccable degree of accuracy is required; this applies to situations where the research is likely to be the subject of close review and scrutiny. When so much relies on the gathering and findings of a researcher, it is most likely best to let seasoned professionals be at the forefront of the research to ensure maximum knowledge and credibility.

> *There are many research options that managers would do well to incorporate into their quest for improving and growing their businesses.*

That being said, there are still many marketing decisions that do not require such a high level of sophistication or technique. In these situations, managers and the companies they represent could significantly benefit from calculated, thorough market studies. There are many research options that managers would do well to incorporate into their quest for improving and growing their businesses. Thus, we begin by tackling the more common misunderstandings of marketing research and exposing them for the misinformation that they are.

COMMON MISUNDERSTANDINGS OF MARKETING RESEARCH

"Market Research Costs Too Much Money and Time"

The idea that market research is simply too expensive is a very common misunderstanding by management. The unfounded notion that high-cost research is the only kind of research that exists, is in part, because of the perception that it is labor intensive and driven by highly trained professionals. This misunderstanding is further perpetuated by the idea that marketing research requires complex surveys in order to obtain necessary data, ultimately used in the analysis. While it is true that valid and reliable surveys can be expensive, there are many other approaches that can more than meet the firm's needs at a much lower cost. As with anything, common sense and a focused thought process can go a long way in helping find ways to reduce costs while still turning out a quality end product.

"Research Will Not Help My Firm"

Sometimes a manager's personal motives can cloud the decision to, or not to, undertake a marketing research program. If a manager believes this type of action may result in an unnecessary waste of time and resources, he will opt to forego the research. This manager perceives that the issues his firm deals with are outside the realm of research and that any additional research conclusions will not help. This may be in the area of pricing, logistics, or product development and are not considered "market research territory."

Unfortunately, this scenario has become increasing problematic. The spectrum of decisions, supported by targeted research is limitless. Today, many firms not only use research to tackle traditional areas of business, such as advertising and sales, but they also use marketing research internally, assessing corporate culture and performance, strengths and weaknesses, and core competencies. Appropriate research questions can be posed at any level of the organization and answered by data collection, analysis, and inference.

"My Current Research Program Is Good Enough"

Many managers believe they are already conducting enough marketing research as a natural consequence of their organization's current activities and involvements. This scenario is similar to the previous misunderstanding in that the perception of the manager is the underlying driver of the research decision. They look around and see performance data and analyses, and more, claiming that as evidence of their argument. While readily available information pools may be potentially useful, it is more likely that they will be of little use when examining specific organizational questions. Furthermore, less experienced personnel may attempt to "make the data" fit the problem, in an effort to be efficient.

Too much data, even if it is the right kind of data, can mask what is truly important, leaving the manager at a loss for direction, while at the same time convincing them that their company is clearly doing plenty of research and analysis already. In many cases, the research may actually be missing the mark, and the researcher will need to create a new program that is targeted towards those unique goals and needs.

Too much data, even if it is the right kind of data, can mask what is truly important...

Simply hoping that existing statistics will be sufficient is not enough. If the information on hand is not carefully cultivated to help make both short and long-term company decisions, it should not be classified as research and should be revamped to make room for a data collection process that brings in information that will truly benefit the company.

"We Only Need to Do Research to Support Major Decisions"

Managers often feel they cannot justify the level of financial output that many serious marketing research programs require since their decisions are minor when compared to those made by larger, more influential companies. The concern is that there are many situations where inconsequential decisions can be greatly improved by a small amount of marketing research that usually can be achieved at minimal cost. In addition, there are many situations in which management does not use marketing research, because they believe that they already have a firm understanding of the problem and the best course of action. More plainly, management does not see the relationship between marketing research and certain decision types.

If marketing research will provide clearer insight or strategic direction for the company, then it should be utilized.

The notion that only major decisions warrant marketing research typically comes from the general practice that managers want to feel "good" about their decisions and need to be able to justify these decisions to superiors. Decision scope and ramifications should not be the ultimate determination when research is undertaken. More importantly, the type of decision should be the driving factor. If marketing research will provide clearer insight or strategic direction for the company, then it should be utilized.

"My Influence as a Manager Will Diminish with More Research"

This misunderstanding perpetuates the idea that many managers hold, believing marketing research is an elite activity to which only a few "academics" are engaged. Managers do not trust their own ability to understand what research they can perform themselves and what research is best procured from outside servicers. If a situation arises where outside research is necessary, many managers move slowly and cautiously simply because they are afraid to let other specialists control the activity.

If new information is allowed to enter the decision equation, and only certain outside people have access to this expert information, then it is those outsiders and not the manager who controls things, keeping the manager inferior to the researcher. This is particularly evident when the research results run against the manager's own views. In addition, many managers worry that outside researchers will overlook the practical realities facing the organization. This is especially true if the manager happens to have an introductory knowledge of research and statistics. College level courses normally serve as a basic preface for the research environment, and can often be intimidating, presenting a snapshot of the complexities.

"Market Research Is Just an Elaborate Term for Taking Surveys"

Many well-meaning managers view marketing research as synonymous with surveys, requiring the same basic resources and concluding the same statistical generalities. The truth of the matter is that there are a wide variety of research techniques that utilize many approaches and a diversity of results. For example, archival examination, simple observation, and low-cost experimentation as opposed to surveys can generate rich data and results and are appropriate research tools under certain circumstances. Normally, the manager has been on the receiving end of surveys and equates his experience as a survey participant with the concept of marketing research. As a participant, it was most likely conveyed to the manager that the survey exercise was "market research" in an effort to analyze quality, perceptions and experiences, or something along those lines.

"Marketing Research Will Solve All of My Sales Problems"

While most of the concerns of undertaking marketing research are negative, in terms of effort, resources, and understanding, a final misunderstanding is also quite common. Inexperienced managers can believe that marketing research will solve a firm's poor performance, primarily in sales. Often, younger industry professionals, recently out of college, will immediately suggest that if more research and statistics were available, the firm could quickly turn those into fast revenues. If revenues are dropping off, managers may hire a research staff or a firm, on a short-term basis, in an effort to quickly right the ship. This approach can be costly, as little attention is paid to the integration of the marketing research with the firm's overall strategy and competitive position. Moreover, an organization's problems may not be correctable by research alone.

COMMON MARKETING RESEARCH USES

Referred to in Chapter One, the four most common uses for marketing research are:

1. identifying market opportunities and problems;
2. generating, refining, and evaluating potential market actions;
3. monitoring market performance; and
4. improving the marketing process.

Identifying market opportunities suggests that the goal of these types of research programs is to find opportunities or to identify problems with an existing strategy or approach. Some examples of these would be market segment identification, product-service use studies, or competitive analysis.

Generating, refining, and evaluating potential market actions can be either broad or narrow in scope. Normally the focus is on some aspect of the marketing mix. Some research examples are new product testing, price testing, or promotional effectiveness.

Monitoring market performance allows firms with marketing programs already in place to evaluate how well they are doing. These may be tracking studies, stakeholder satisfaction studies, or image analysis.

Improving the marketing process is macro-based research focused not on specific problems facing the company, but rather an effort to understand the overall marketing procedures. Buyer behavior and decision-making process awareness, implementing new products policies, or examining marketing expenditures against firm performance are some examples. By having this knowledge, managers will be in a much better position to solve specific problems with their firms.

This book's main goal is to inform, prepare, teach, and inspire managers to be better stewards of the research tools and resources that are at their disposal.

WHAT'S NEXT?

This book was written as a direct response to the concerns discussed above. It is a book about affordable marketing research that is written for both present and future marketing professionals and managers, as well as for firms and managers with limited resources and little to no understanding of how to properly use and benefit from information once it has been collected. Ultimately, this book's main goal is to inform, prepare, teach, and inspire managers to be better stewards of the research tools and resources that are at their disposal. As active consultants, we know there is no substitute for experience!

This book teaches managers, as well as other individuals, to determine when marketing research would be a benefit to them, even if their resources may be few or if the decisions they are looking to support are important, yet not necessarily life changing. It also provides a functional framework or approach that ensures the data gathered are both relevant and usable and further evaluates a wide range of techniques geared toward conducting resource-friendly research that is still high quality.

The flow of the chapters in this book is simple, linear, and forthright. Chapters three and four set up the research problem and introduce the functional approach to marketing research. This approach is straightforward, offering the manager a logical approach to efficient and effective research. Chapters five through eight address data collection, from using secondary data and simple observational approaches to more complex primary data by use of survey engagement. Chapters nine and ten provide insight into understanding your data findings and, furthermore, what the results suggest about your organizational questions. Lastly, Chapter eleven provides the culmination of putting the research program into an understandable product and preparing for the action steps ahead.

RECURRING CASE SCENARIO

As a matter of efficiency and effectiveness, there will be a recurring applied scenario from time to time throughout the book. The introduction and background will be provided here, and then as new topics are developed, conditions and questions regarding the business will be addressed as an example. This is the place where real, practical work is done. This is "on the ground."

Matt Brown and his family own Everything Automotive. The store would be described as a typical auto parts store with expert consulting service. The company has been in the family since 1958, originally started by his grandfather, Joe Brown. There are currently three different locations: Mountainview, Meadow Valley, and Hildale. Mountainview is the north location and is about 35 miles from Meadow Valley. Consequently, Hildale is located about 20 miles to the south of Meadow Valley. Matt's managing director is Mark Jones, and each of the locations has an onsite manager. Everything Automotive (EA) has been part of the Independent Auto Parts Association for the last 25 years, and this has allowed them to stay somewhat competitive with the large chains of today. As of 2017, Mountainview has been enjoying a six percent profit on average over the last five years; Meadow Valley's profit has been zero percent during that same time, while the Hildale location has been losing about two percent.

Matt Brown believes it is now time to make some decisions as to the future viability and direction of EA. He feels the company has become out of touch with its customers and less competitive with product offerings. Therefore, he has decided to undertake a comprehensive marketing research campaign with an attempt to properly position his product and become more profitable. His primary questions right now are:

- Who are our customers?
- How do our customers differ at the different locations?
- What are our customers' preferences and habits?
- How do we get and keep more customers?
- What advertising approach should we be using?

These are the big questions. As we move forward through the book, more questions will inevitably appear.

Chapter 3

THE RESEARCH AGENDA

Marketing research is such an integral part of management that it must be led intentionally and appropriately, and not left to chance. Like most duties of a manager, research programs and opportunities must be planned in order to be effective. Committing to this requires organizations to appreciate research and to decide to perform that research in a consistent and systematic manner. Thankfully, options for marketing research may be more widespread than previously anticipated. It is crucial that even people without a background in research techniques incorporate research methods into their daily work.

It is important to note that this planning process should not be done in secrecy.

THE RESEARCH PLAN

Before an organization begins to coordinate studies on a yearly basis, a correct framework needs to be put in place. One good thing to do would be to document the types of marketing decisions that frequently occur in the organization for managers to reference in the future. This includes actions that keep the current state, not just choices that may shake up the present practices, procedures, or approaches. Performing this simple step will set the stage for identifying what information is required to make those decisions more effective. A list of potential research projects must also be generated. This list can be a valuable tool, if ordered by priority, which will be frequently referenced. Doing this will create a methodology that can be engaged in the future to help decide if new decisions are warranted and if any changes need to be made to the existing research programs.

It is important to note that this planning should not occur in secrecy. In an attempt to synergize efforts, it makes sense for the entire organization to be on board with the tasks and decisions to be made.

---

1. Identify tasks and decisions for the upcoming planning period.
2. Recognize roadblocks for these tasks and decisions.
3. Determine the information needed to support the tasks and decisions stipulated in step 1.
4. Achieve consensus on the priority of tasks and decisions.
5. Estimate a budget and timeframe for task and decision completion.
6. Ensure that the entire organization is aware of the tasks and decisions to be made.
7. Establish viable and measurable controls to gauge the success of the tasks and decisions.

Figure 3.1. A Common Research Planning Approach.

Research results will often be usable by multiple departments who have slightly different perspectives for the use and value of the information.

THE DECISION FRAMEWORK

Though most management decisions are made by individuals, most marketing decisions will utilize data from the same three categories:

1. Decisions that are made will either be short or long-range. Managers must frequently look to future planning sessions to determine into which category the specific decision fits.
2. Specifically define tactics and strategies. Long-term decision-making is usually more strategic: identifying whom to target, deciding on the goods and services to sell, determining how to approach the target audience successfully, and developing the organizational structure, systems, and staff to make it all happen. While short-range decisions typically deal with tactical issues such as deciding on audience segments, they sometimes focus on strategic questions. For example, this may be developing a new product line or location.
3. Determine if decisions are related to direct components of the marketing mix (goods and services offered, price structure, ads, public relations efforts, etc.) or, conversely, outside factors that are necessary to the marketing effort.

These three categories of choices contribute to the initial foundation that is required at the beginning of a yearly planned course of action.

Firm	Market
• Firm Data	• Product Offerings
• Employees	• Pricing
• Contractors	• Consumer Patterns
• Competitors	• Promotional Distinctives
• Firm Capabilities	• Online Activity
	• Distribution Alternatives

Figure 3.2. Research Planning Resource Potential.

INFORMATION TYPES

For sound decision-making (specifically regarding whether to leave things in the state in which they currently are or to modify the different elements that comprise the current marketing mix) management has to identify the cause-and-effect links between the data they are receiving and all outcomes, both positive and negative.

This means finding the answers to many questions:

Explanatory Information - this informative data, posed as questions and answers, is most valuable during short-term decision making.

- Queries regarding factors outside management's control, such as: Do differences in social and monetary conditions impact us as an organization? How do you think this happens? Are the goals, personal preferences, and attitudes of the system partners and consumers influencing how effective our marketing practices are? Why do you think this is?
- Questions on things under management's control, such as: Does the nature and degree of the marketing mix greatly impact our marketing effectiveness? If this is the case, how? If this is not the case, why not?
- Questions that address changes in the market, such as: What factors make our current results fall in or out of line with previous ones? How is the program environment changing these days? How will this decision impact us in the following year? What about over the course of five or ten years?

Descriptive Information - one way to define these opportunities is to perform a marketing audit. The market environment is made up of:

- Consumers: Find out who responds positively to your marketing efforts and who does not. What do they like, how do they feel, what do they want to do when they see what you have to offer?
- Competition: Where is your audience turning to as an alternative to your product? Evaluate your competitors and determine what marketing strategies they utilize, how much money they spend, and who their target audience is.

- Channels: Where are your target groups running across your offerings as well as that of your rivals? How satisfied are the partners you utilize with the relationship you have established? How much does the distribution system cost? Can the Internet be utilized for delivery of the project options?
- Marketing system performance: How well are your assorted projects doing? Can they take care of themselves? Are you aware of their trends?
- Money and societal environments: What is the status of general social acceptance or non-acceptance of the company's offerings or marketing approaches?

How is each target audience surviving the current socio-economic state? These questions will allow an organization to determine what is required to manage effectively: foreseeing possible future events sensibly, with solid support and careful consideration. The manager's activities during planning will result in consequences, some good and some bad, so it is imperative that the manager is able to foresee future events so that the project can stay on track.

Predictive Information – Those questions and their corresponding answers are usually most valuable for strategic decisions with long-term significant, detailed information. Management wants to learn about the market environment in its present state.

Because planning always takes place in an environment of uncertainty, it has never been seen as easy, and most managers know that is true in today's economy more than ever.

You may not get the whole story from the above questions and the descriptive and explanatory information their answers provide, so you may need to ask more questions to gather enough information for forecasting purposes:

- Questions focusing on the possible strategies and tactics that company partners may employ, thus affecting the company's future operations, such as: If the organization does not change its direction, will it financially thrive and will the staff and systems employed be able to keep abreast of any future change and growth?
- Queries relating to any possible major developments in the outside political and social arenas that might create possible setbacks to the organization, such as: What will technology appear to be in the future? Are there existing communication system developments or Internet options that may positively or negatively impact our daily operations or even our service or product offerings? The manager must always monitor the task and general environment for changes in order to identify opportunities and threats that may require decisions. Changes in the nature, number, or types of customers, competitors, suppliers, or distributors constantly have an impact on the business and its need for daily decisions. Managers must ask questions and consistently analyze forces in the general environment (economic forces, technology changes, socio-cultural forces, demographic changes, and political and/or legal forces that affect ongoing planning and decision-making. Political decisions regarding taxes, imports, exports, regulations, etc. cannot be evaluated in a reactionary posture – they must be anticipated and predicted.

MOVING FORWARD

The reader may be overwhelmed by how complicated the research planning process appears, particularly when there are multiple projects and decisions being considered. Remember, difficult situations do not need to be avoided. Because planning always takes place in an environment of uncertainty, it has never been seen as easy, and most managers know that is true in today's economy more than ever. The manager must make individual sacrifices if he or she hopes to be an effective leader. Successful managers do not consider their responsibilities small enough to handle extemporaneously or on the spur of the moment. They must have a keen awareness and understanding of the environment which their organization is working in – both inside and outside – and then they carefully and systematically apply the knowledge to plan effectively, both for the present and the future.

Of course, there are situations where managers use common sense or gut feelings to make decisions; they will move forward without doing research because the decision does not warrant using financial resources or there are no viable or logical research opportunities. Nonetheless, effective managers must ensure that snap judgments are only made once they have determined - without a doubt - that collecting research is either not necessary or not achievable. You should think of this as the research plan's primary objective. It may be difficult planning this task the first time, but the manager can rest assured that future planning cycles will be much easier.

DEVELOPING THE INITIAL RESEARCH PLAN

At the start, all key management staff who might be helpful should be part of the planning process. This is not exclusive to management personnel and high-ranking staff; the company may employ others whose insight and capabilities might be helpful during the planning stage. Those people who may conduct the actual research, or who may utilize the knowledge gained as a result of that research, should be included as well. During the early planning stages, a consultation from an outside adviser will be beneficial for the market research community. They can offer new, creative options that managers and other employees may not think of, which will expand the company's knowledge base significantly.

The success of this meeting and the planning period as a whole rests upon the ability to block time for the meeting early in the planning process. At least for the first pass, the blocked time should be free of distractions or requirements. Research meetings that are located out of the office may be more effective and productive, depending on what locations you have available between the offices.

Each research category should be covered independently, beginning with long-range strategic needs like the ones mentioned in Exhibit 3.1, followed by short-range strategies and tactics. The leading manager must ensure that each and every category is thoroughly reviewed, particularly during the first meeting. All participants require briefing on the purpose of planning, basically developing a "want list." Participants should be encouraged to drop their inhibitions and openly state their wants and concerns. Remember, at this stage in the game, ruling out research opportunities would be irresponsible, as the company's budget and research options will be analyzed later.

PRIORITIZING

Take a break and gather your thoughts, then pursue the next phase, which is considering the tasks and decisions on the research planning list and categorizing them by priority.

- *High Priority:* This group will list those projects that appear to be doable, necessary, and worthy of having funds allocated to them this year.
- *Medium Priority:* Projects which are considered doable but not so important that they deserve a quick funding guarantee. Those projects are still near the top of the company's wish list, however, and should be continually checked on during the entire year.

- *Low Priority:* These are projects that are not crucial but would be a benefit and are often easily achievable. Management should keep its eye out for free or inexpensive opportunities to gather data. This category would also include projects that would ordinarily be found in the High Priority group, but the organization lacks the information, skills, financial resources, or staff to make them feasible.

Knowing that management would allocate finances to certain projects if they could verifiably close the knowledge gaps or gain access to the right materials and staff, there should be a concerted effort to identify the means to get these projects going. To evaluate future project options, you can send out a "Request for Proposal" to local suppliers of research or consultants.

The final priority category is:

- *Non-Priority:* These are projects that might have belonged in the Medium Priority group, but right now are not a real possibility and are not at the top of the list. In addition, non-priority projects are those not practical to complete given methodological limitations.

The final purpose of research planning is to set up a timetable and a detailed budget to complete category High Priority projects. In this stage, various activities will also begin that help advance these projects further. The manager should also start exploring how beneficial deferring projects would be. A "watch list" of all category Medium Priority projects would be valuable to those in the company who are considering becoming involved in research sometime in the future.

FUTURE ACTIVITY

Ideally, once the study creation process is finished, it can be taken into consideration in the future, thus causing the organizing for that year to be broken down and simpler to follow. A great way of moving forward for looking over the current plan would be to inquire about things like:

- Which of past research projects are finished and do not need to be revisited, at least for a bit?
- Which project do you think is irrelevant enough to be deleted?
- Select new projects to be included.
- Which project of ours is valuable or successful enough to be repeated? Will they look and be operated the same as those in the past?
- What projects should be updated based on new information or underlying circumstances that have come forward since their inception?

Another step that would be effective to add after the first year would be a regular review of the planning process. Someone, whether a qualified manager or an outside consultant, should assess research decisions from last year and determine if and how the planning process could be shortened or improved.

You should be able to answer questions regarding whether or not categorizing systems were effective and appropriate or whether they had to be reorganized on a regular basis. Ask:

- Could you have anticipated those reassignments based on the planning process itself? If yes, what would be the best approach to add to the planning process to handle those anticipations?
- Could we have anticipated any new wants that have come up in the past year?

This is all reliant on a regular evaluation of process for research planning. The next chapter reviews the evaluation process for each individual research project based on its specific criteria.

IDENTIFYING RESEARCH OPPORTUNITIES

Because managers typically do not understand the value or recognize worthwhile, inexpensive research opportunities, the companies often lose out on those opportunities. First, there may be many opportunities that are not noticed because the manager is unaware of research capabilities. Second, there may be options that are not thoroughly reviewed because the manager does not take the time. Third, many managers are blind to research opportunities as they do not strive to intentionally, constantly, and methodically look into them.

> *This research planning process ensures that the organization is making the most responsible, appropriate, evidence-based marketing decisions.*

This procedure describes a systematic method for identifying research needs and handling unanticipated research alternatives. Although the entire setup may be difficult the first time, taking advantage of opportunities for low-cost research will help the company rise above the competition and the investment of time in this process will provide a long-term return. This research planning process ensures that the organization is making the most responsible, appropriate, evidence-based marketing decisions.

Measured, concentrated research can greatly assist the manager in making many of his or her daily decisions. It takes a certain way of thinking to become a more effective decision maker using top-notch, low-cost research implements: identifying research goes beyond just being alert; it means having research techniques at your fingertips to use as situations arise. This book provides a variety of techniques that can ease difficulty in decision-making situations. Using research carefully is critical. In the next chapter, we will further detail how managers must look at all options, not just research, when considering your organization's viability and future success.

On the Ground

Let's take our first look at Everything Automotive, and one of the problems facing Matt Brown. EA started a loyalty program two years ago from an idea that came from one of his general managers. On somewhat of a shoestring budget, Matt decided to give customers the opportunity to buy a $10 annual EA Benefits Card which would give the customer discounts on parts and services. Because this was a hurried initiative, the cards were simply paper cards with no electronic tracking. Furthermore, little insight was given to the tracking of cardholder behaviors, or long term risks and returns, as the focus was more on advertising.

At this point, Matt is finding it difficult to determine if the program is working. Specifically, he is looking at his current projects and developing his list of potential new research projects and dividing them into two categories: short-term and long-term. The major initiatives he is considering are:

1. adopting a formal contract alliance program with local mechanics and promoting at the mechanics locations,
2. increase the per sale revenue
3. hold special themed events at store locations
4. start a consumer delivery service

Matt has questions like:

- What products would be good to bundle to increase sales?
- What is the cost benefit of hosting events at the 3 locations?
- What customer segments would attend?
- How do we approach them?
- Who would staff the event?

- What other service benefits would be offered?
- What product items bring the most profit?
- Do I run advertisements and in what media type?
- Should I continue with the current loyalty program?
- How much money is the loyalty program making?

Chapter 4

USING THE FUNCTIONAL APPROACH

Let's assume that you are prepared to invest in a limited program of preplanned research each year and are now open to the possibilities of spontaneous research projects. You and your staff members have together established a place and a time when you will be able to get started on your research project. In this chapter, we will address questions such as: How much time should be spent on a particular research project? What happens when doubts arise about your project? How will you, as a researcher, recognize when your task is finished?

You must first develop your budget. There are a few guidelines to follow when setting a research budget. Some may seem unfounded and others simplistic, yet they are guidelines. One approach is to use the percentage of sales change year over year.

You must first develop your budget.

This approach creates a budget that is based in a concept of proportionality that may be flawed. This approach asks management to decide on a research budget based on a percentage rate of sales. The annual budget may typically be a percentage of the total predicted sales. For one particular project, it could be a percentage of projected sales, too, or of the capital investment.

To illustrate, this could be seen as setting the advertising budget based on a percentage of sales. Whatever percentage was selected might or might not be suitable for the tasks that need to be done. Using this method, advertising funds would be cut just when they are needed to be increased, when sales are down and the market share is competitive; the percentage method would indicate the advertising budget should be cut since the sales totals are down.

Research spending allocation can be seen as following the same logic. If there is a lot at stake, managers think that they have to spend a lot of money, but they think that if there is little at stake, they need not spend a significant amount of money. However, management should always keep in mind that a decision will be made regardless of the value of the research or how much money is spent on it. The results of research realistically change the manager's decision very little - unless the information gathered indicates the decision path was not on the right track. An identical logic would work on a dynamic market. When sales look like they will be good, the business might not worry so much about making a correct decision because they may feel just about anything works in a booming market. In this case, too, research is frequently less able to be justified. Conversely, when sales are low, managers might be quite anxious to make the right decision. In such instances, even for very small company decisions, the value of research increases.

THE APPROACH OF AFFORDABILITY (RESIDUAL APPROACH)

The percentage of sales approach is often performed so that organization is certain that the desired research fits in their budget. Affordable residual research is considered a necessary and valuable component of business. The percentage of sales approach considers research a discretionary item that may or may not be purchased with profits from the product. In addition, this approach tends to skew the research budget even more radically than when it is based on the sales curve of the business. If sales drop even a little, a manager could very well panic and slash the budget for research in order to try to make sure the company's bottom line stays intact. Conversely, discretionary cash might rise quickly when sales are good. The problem of budget that can be seen in percentage and affordable strategies means that it is almost impossible to have a consistent flow of research.

A market rate approach is yet another way to set the research budget. This usually results from a manager being naive regarding what it actually takes to make a good decision. Most of the time, it creates a problem for the supplier of the research as an additional burden to the budget with a research proposal. When this situation is at an extreme, managers may feel that it is best to seek competitive bids for the project rather than manage it themselves. In this way, the cost of research is reduced in the process of bidding. If a Request for Proposal (RFP) is posted for the project and several organizations bid, the proposals will give the manager a better idea of realistic research costs. This leads to the manager basing the decision on the cost of the research rather than the quality of the research as well as the feeling that they have explored every possible avenue of keeping costs down while still solving the issue.

The main fallacy in this popularly employed method is that the manager expects the bidding process to magically work out in some way because the decision to outsource the project has been made. The reality is that cost-determination processes are affected by available technology, external market forces, and supplier bidding policies. When this sort of problem is sent out for bids, some of the proposals may be very odd and seem underpriced, while others may be quite expensive. This may be the result of some vendors making use of new technology or they have a great deal of experience and can do the work much more efficiently. If the manager has not planned well for the needs of the company, many great opportunities may be missed. Clearly, in this type of situation it is uncertain whether or not the bid chosen will be right for the manager's budget or of an appropriate sort for the manager's decision. Nonetheless, it is not wise to choose researchers based on cost alone. A manager has to take great care to decide on every proposal based on the experience and background of each researcher as well as the references he or she can provide.

OTHER ISSUES FOR CONSIDERATION

A good number of other factors exist which impact a budget and make it fluctuate, such as the following conditions:

Customer Relations

Of course, questionnaires and detailed interviews are done to gather data, but a secondary benefit is that they let the customers and other outsiders speak their minds and feel part of the process. A good vendor may survey a larger than required group of subjects. This act of going the extra mile may result in unexpected trust and goodwill between the firm and the vendor. One good example might be a college that opts to ask opinions of every incoming freshman as opposed to a smaller focus group. This simple action may be done in order to foster positive student/college relations.

Necessities Due to Outside Political Realities

Studies are often overly extensive due to a misplaced wish to ensure everything is covered during the research process. That most frequently happens in cases where the information is going to be used in a lawsuit or a regulatory environment.

Inside Political Requirements

When uncertainty occurs, researchers rush to uncover the problem. This can cause a rise in research budgets.

Proper Use of Rhetoric

If there are disagreements within the organization itself, it might be necessary to create a larger study than one would statistically need in order to validate the findings of the researcher or manager. One statewide public health agency phone survey was conducted using a sample size of 500. This size was chosen because it was a typical size according to prevailing wisdom. In many cases, a smaller sampling would yield the same results; however, a larger sampling is more impressive.

BUILDING A BUDGET BASED ON THE DECISION

The previous scenarios showed us what not to do; however, this does not tell us what we should do. The easiest thing is to start with the decision(s) that need to be made, which means that the managers and the committee need to have done the work of laying out the end goal. By the time a budget needs to be fixed, everybody involved must clearly comprehend the goal and has to be prepared to put their money where their vision is.

GIVING THE DECISION STRUCTURE

Which parts of the decision will impact what is spent on a particular research project? The answer to this inquiry deserves a brief visit to the academic universe of decision theory, which is just a structured approach of thinking about management issues.

Every decision has five basic traits:

1. The possible outcome
2. The environment in which the decision takes place
3. Anticipated results
4. How probable future scenarios might be
5. Decision constraints

Decision Options

Initially, decision makers must intuitively outline all the decision alternatives. This creates a simplistic set of expected scenarios that will surface once data is evaluated. It must be clear to the manager what expected paths exist for the organization. For example, should the firm enter a new market or not. This is a simple option choice; however, it is also effective. The posture of the decisions in too complicated a framework will make decisions more difficult.

Decision Setting

Next, it is necessary to determine the fundamental elements of the future scenario that will affect what alternative is chosen and have it gravitate toward being a good choice or a poor one. Those might be factors that management cannot control, such as which direction interest rates will move in the near term or what is the percentage of potential customers who already own their product or a similar one. Or there may be factors that the management can control through the decisions they make in terms of advertising, budget, or other policy decisions. Some environmental influences will be difficult to predict and hence complicates future planning.

Expected Results

The manager needs to anticipate a result for every possible combination of a decision choice and a future environmental scenario. Typically, the result will come with a financial perspective that pertains to the potential consequences of doing this within a specific environment, such as listing the net profit before taxes. In nonprofits, such results can be put in alternate ways, such as votes for a candidate or the number of people who might opt to engage in a particular behavior or habit.

The Probabilities that Various Scenarios Might Occur

After working in the field for years, many managers tend to have gut feelings and usually see the future from their particular perspective. Formal decision theory simply requires management to see all of these estimates and projections as potentially probable. The most probable outcomes of a decision are usually addressed with the use of this theory.

The manager and the planning team should now come to a consensus about a rule or set of rules that will be able to lead them to the selection of a decision path.

A Decision Procedure

This multi-faceted approach that includes alternative plans, future scenarios, results, and intuitive projections combines the elements that are needed to reach the final decision. The manager and the planning team should now come to a consensus about a rule or set of rules that will be able to lead them to the selection of a decision path. The team may consider a number of different rule options. On the flip side, there are two decision rules that are best avoided.

Not Holding Back

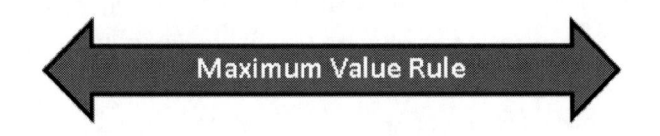

⬅ **Maximum Value Rule** ➡

This rule suggests that a manager selects an action plan that, in comparison to every other possible scenario, may very well produce the one best result. That is a rule most beneficial to gamblers and organizations that gamble on one-time huge payoffs. The biggest problem with this rule is that it often ignores any possible negative future scenarios and rather opts to concentrate on the positive side of any decision or prospective result.

Not Risking Too Much

This second rule shifts to the opposite end of decision making - looking at the worst possible result within each action plan and choosing the one that is likely to cause the least amount of potential problems. This rule is usually followed by highly conservative groups or by businesses whose budget is so tight that they know they would not be able to survive if they lost even a bit of money. This is generally not a successful strategy as it focuses solely on the negatives of the issue instead of considering the positives as well.

In the middle of the two extremes is found the "maximum value rule." This rule means the manager can weigh possible results of every decision that could be made and involves the probabilities of any potential future environment. In doing this, the best plan of action emerges as the one that looks as if it might facilitate the best results out of all possibilities in the future. Doing this will not automatically guarantee success, but over the long term, it will provide you with the highest average payoffs.

Naturally, no manager can conduct a study completely without flaws, which makes us ask what he or she needs to do about putting time and money into a less than perfect research project.

COST UNCERTAINTY FACTORS

Two factors have a direct effect on the cost of uncertainty. The most important factor is the investment associated with the decision. Expansion of the financial or influential features can increase the uncertainty and risk associated with that decision.

Another concern is the issue of whether or not to conduct research, which is difficult for any manager to decide. That is one question that leads to many smaller ones, such as the amount to spend, who should be involved, and much more. Naturally, no manager can conduct a study completely without flaws, which makes us ask what he or she needs to do about putting time and money into a less than perfect research project. In this sort of example, the first thing to do is to find out if the information you seek may be gathered as outlined above for the price of uncertainty. Because that serves as the upper limit as to what can be spent on research, it is an easy way to check whether a study is really feasible.

There are techniques a manager may feel are beneficial to his or her organization at a reasonable cost. After that, the question arises as to the amount of money that needs to be set aside so the research can happen. This is most often answered using common sense and experience as opposed to utilizing decision theory or a computer analysis program in order to allocate funds to the project.

Keep in mind that while it is easy to demonstrate costs in monetary terms, there are others consequences to the decision-making process. For example, the risks a bad decision poses to one's career or the credibility of the organization and even the possibility of legal repercussions. The consequences are hard to predict, but it is still essential to consider other types of outcomes when making a decision. It could even be wise to place a dollar value on such results to be able to see a more thorough picture of what financial factors will be involved in the decision. For example, as a way of reflecting the positive effects that research might have on a project, managers might provide a payoff consideration of around $1,000.

Additional factors that may cause resistance of the research: There is a notion that research should be used only when companies and managers truly understand the benefit of it. This can be a bit dangerous. The first thing is that a manager might lean towards an excessive amount of research if it is found that there are strategies that are affordable and easy to do. Such a cavalier attitude toward collecting huge amounts of research data may sometimes result in wasted resources. Another downside to this is that it can lead management to believe that research, however affordable, does not yield practical or useful information, and thus it should not be carried out.

Two things should be kept in mind about research campaigns. First, if there is no obvious benefit of the research and no decisions hover around some expected outcome, then do not waste the time. Research for research sake is counterproductive. Second, if research is warranted, stay away from the data trap. Many inexperienced researchers will suggest that you gather large amounts of data, both in samples and variables. This approach becomes cumbersome and more expensive than necessary and can often cause confusion when interpreting the results. Stick to a feasible and affordable plan.

Research should only be performed with a clear benefit in mind.

Many situations also exist which should exclude research:

- Avoid research if its only aim is to overcome personal insecurities. If a manager has done the groundwork and followed the outlined decision framework to find that it is not rational to do research, obviously, he or she should not proceed with a research project as a form of a security blanket.

- Do not conduct research if its only aim is to defend a particular decision to other people in the company. Do not carry out research on the off chance that it may become necessary for political reasons, even though experience may indicate that rival managers and bosses might insist on backup research before taking action.
- Do not research something if the only reason is to track something. A fiscally savvy manager will keep his or her eyes peeled for useful data since it is wasteful to spend research dollars on information that is free.
- Avoid conducting research that is essentially a wild goose chase. Research should only be performed with a clear benefit in mind. If there is no clear rationale behind the study, think twice before conducting it.
- Do not implement research that is merely meant to satisfy a manager's curiosity. Many wasteful research projects have begun with an idle curiosity about something it would be interesting to know about. Managers need effective, proven results, not simply the most intriguing ones.
- Do not implement research that is fed by a desire to outdo colleagues or the competition. It is particularly true of research fads which may gain a big following but may not be right for everybody. Letting that temptation take hold will probably result in resources being wasted and results that are not satisfactory.
- Avoid research when it is done for the sole enjoyment of the research activity. Too frequently managers jump on a project that excites them and start research strategies without being patient enough to decide if they will indeed serve the purposes of the study or the company itself. Spending time and money to collect answers to fascinating questions without taking action is a colossal waste of resources.

FAULTY RESEARCH

Our sympathies are with this manager (owner, senior executive, etc.), but this person must take some of the blame for the study that is poorly designed. The manager made the common mistake of not collaborating fully with the researcher in this endeavor. Whether research is a success or a failure is contingent upon the strength of collaboration between the manager and the researcher. It is crucial that the manager openly and honestly express the priorities of the research so the proper research frame can be developed.

The initial step is to define the problem. After this, the problem is translated into research methodology. What follows is the development of research instruments, sampling plans, interviewing instructions, coding and various other details. A researcher goes into the field, looks at the data that is found, and reports the findings in written form. This standard method of approach is detailed in Figure 4.1.

1. Define the Research Problem
2. Examine Secondary Resources Available
3. Design a Primary Research Plan
4. Identify Necessary Resources Required for the Research
5. Design the Survey Instrument
6. Identify the Population and Sampling Approach
7. Carry out Research
8. Analyze Collected Data
9. Draw Conclusions from Collected Data
10. Disseminate Results in a Written Report

Figure 4.1. Traditional Research Approach.

The manager then assembles and evaluates the researcher's reports and converts them into the next steps - specifically, how they will be applied. Generally speaking, the scope of the research should remain general prior to the start of the research, rather than overly specific. A manager will usually define the problem to be researched as a wide area of which he or she is ignorant. Managers are effectively admitting that there are things they do not know about a situation, such as: "I'll have more information after I see the results; I can make a decision once I know more." This often leads to ineffective and inefficient decision making.

Our recommended method is more innovative, but it ends up with more effective, usable results. This is a procedure stressing close cooperation between decision makers in the organization and researchers. This procedure increases the likelihood that company representatives will end up with findings that are both actionable and interesting.

A FUNCTIONAL APPROACH TO MARKETING RESEARCH

1.	Bring key managers together
2.	Identify high priority tasks and decisions that need to be made
3.	Establish consensus on the final priority of the research projects
4.	Identify what research results will assist management with their key tasks and decisions
5.	Reaffirm that research results will lead to the implementation of tasks and decisions
6.	Determine what research and statistical analysis will be required to support the priority tasks and decisions
7.	Create questions that support the research and ultimate desired outcome
8.	Verify if the questions have already been answered, or if similar data already exists
9.	Decide on the population and sample to be examined
10.	Carry out the research
11.	Analyze the data
12.	Draft a written report to disseminate among key managers
13.	Bring key managers together to examine findings
14.	Implement tasks and make decisions based on findings
15.	Determine a future time to evaluate implemented tasks and decisions
16.	Evaluate results of priority tasks and decisions

Figure 4.2. A Functional Approach to Marketing Research.

This out of the box thinking method starts where the process usually ends and works back from there. The logical or "functional" approach in every phase of the process leads to what comes after it and is not dependent on what has gone before it.

Figure 4.2 outlines this approach and each step is examined thereafter.

1. Bring Key Managers Together

Although this seems like a logical first step, it is often overlooked. There is usually a key decision maker who is championing the research agenda, and this individual, either purposefully or by accident, leaves out key company individuals in the research process. There are numerous specific reasons for this; however, the bottom line is that all key decision makers from the various organizational function come together to explore the upcoming research project.

2. Identify High Priority Tasks and Decisions That Need to Be Made

Determine what decisions must be made. Managers often perceive that the problems with their research are due to a lack of information in regards to the current market. This allows the solution to become the extremely simple process of making what is known become what is known.

3. Establish Consensus on the Final Priority of the Research Projects

After the exploratory phase, a critical step is to come to an organizational consensus of what key decisions and tasks need to be addressed in the research project. It is important to be acutely aware of those decision makers that appear apathetic, uncomfortable, or simply against the research direction the firm is going. This will be important later as results become known.

4. Identify What Research Results Will Assist Management with Their Key Tasks and Decisions

Identify the necessary information for successful conversations with management. This will help to determine what sort of language is necessary to convey the possible choices of action. In order to increase the odds that the correct course will be selected, it may be best to offer multiple choice answers. Hypothetically present expected findings so that key players will understand where the research is going and what is expected in the end. The key players need to confirm that the research about to be undertaken is in fact the correct information.

5. Reaffirm That Research Results Will Lead to the Implementation of Tasks and Decisions

One way to come up with useful report material is to treat the situation as if it were a case study. In this step, it is important to create a prototype report in which management finds out how the final report will look. This way management will clearly understand each of the action steps to be taken to attain the goal. Doing this allows the research team to collaborate effectively with the manager, resulting in a particularly creative project.

Remember that when managers participate in this very necessary and very valuable hypothetical thinking phase of the process of backward research, there is much to be gained. For example:

- Managers may feel encouraged to stick up for research work if it is later criticized.
- It helps the manager understand the details of how the research works and it also helps people appreciate its benefits and also its weaknesses.
- This engenders anticipation within the manager so he or she is prepared to utilize the research findings as they manifest.
- It minimizes the possibility that a manager will be shocked with completely surprising results.
- It will show any interested manager what possible limitations there could be to the study.

6. Determine What Research and Statistical Analysis Will Be Required to Support the Priority Tasks and Decisions

The type of analysis will be determined in large part by the form the report will take. There are times when certain types of research can be too complex for management to understand. If the manager feels at ease with complicated statistics, the researcher can similarly prolong a number of the more complicated analytic steps. Generally, however, this phase of analysis needs to be as direct as it can be. In the ideal situation when the writing of the hypothetical table has done what it was supposed to do, an analysis will hardly be more work than just filling in the blanks.

7. Create Questions That Support the Research and Ultimate Desired Outcome

In the phase of data gathering, it is best to work logically and decide the kind of information that needs to be gathered as well as to decide on the wording of the questions. Phrasing the questions is a key step that needs detailed attention. Make sure the questions being answered are those that you really need. Also, include some specifics on who is answering.

8. Verify If the Questions Have Already Been Answered, or If Similar Data Already Exists

Find out if the information already exists somewhere. It is easy to do and can help the manager in the beginning of the research process. The increase of marketing research as well as the Internet has made accessing secondary information sources much easier. Numerous examples are provided in the Appendix.

9. Decide on the Population and Sample to Be Examined

Next, using this type of functional approach, you can determine the best way to use probability sampling techniques. Researchers often generate an inadequate or an excessive amount of sampling for use in their investigation. Doing it this way sets firm boundaries and a clear course of action which is understandable to both managers and the researcher. In a similar way, writing a scenario will show that management may need a more complex breakdown of the outcome than the researcher thinks will be required so as to allow the research to more fully meet the needs of the manager. Also, specifically identify what target group or population group you want to gather information from, such as customers, employees, etc.

10. Carry Out the Research

Gather the data needed for the research project. This may be in the form of surveys, focus groups, intercepts, or a similar technique. It is imperative that at some point, the population is sampled. Diligence is required to ensure that you are indeed questioning the population of the study. This is typically the most time-consuming step.

> *The data itself is worthless, however, once the date is analyzed, it will provide fruitful information.*

11. Analyze the Data

In this step, you simply need to process the data gathered in the previous stage. Following the agenda you established early in the process, you will need to complete those statistical techniques that offer the most rich and robust results. The data itself is worthless, however, once the date is analyzed, it will provide fruitful information. More discussion of statistical techniques is discussed later in the book.

12. Draft a Written Report to Disseminate Among Key Managers

Write a report of the findings. Be sure to include the research agenda, specific research questions being addressed, the statistical results to each of the questions and then the conclusions drawn from the data. Once the report is drafted, disseminate the results to the firm's key managers, those in attendance in the beginning of the process. Let them know you will seek their specific feedback on the report.

13. Bring Key Managers Together to Examine Findings

Somewhat similar to step one, you should once again bring all key managers together to discuss the findings after they have had time to review the report. It is important to solicit their thoughts on the findings, trying to determine how decisions are to be supported and what is the next step for the task-oriented items identified in step two.

14. Implement Tasks and Make Decisions Based on Findings

Once all key managers have had a chance to give feedback and express their thoughts, the next step is to begin the implementation of those items supported by the research. Believe it or not, many firms will get to this step, and for some reason they stop! The culture of some firms is noticeably paralyzed when it comes to making decisions or starting new firm programs. It is not uncommon for some firms at this point to "request" more data, demonstrating a lack of confidence in the findings.

15. Determine a Future Time to Evaluate Implemented Tasks and Decisions

Once the implementation of research results is put in play, a measurable timeframe for evaluation is necessary. Based on the decisions to be made and the tasks to be developed, it should be fairly simple for key managers to estimate in what timeframes these actions will occur. These timeframe deadlines should be real and enforced.

16. Evaluate Results of Priority Tasks and Decisions

Lastly, once the research agenda is completed, key managers should again regroup to assess both the process and the results. Will the firm implement a similar agenda in the future? What were the high and low points of the process? Was the data integral to the performance of the decisions and tasks? These are only a few final items to address.

In the final analysis, it seems that traditional approaches may be chosen in hopes that by thoroughly examining a problem the desired outcome will be attained. By using the functional approach, researchers and managers can devise a careful step by step plan to ensure the success of their improvements. Using this functional approach, managers are better able to understand results and use findings immediately. Those working on a tight budget cannot afford just to spend money on projects that are not to the point or cannot be implemented. This functional approach is time intensive, although over the long term it can save money and resources as well as guarantee that the research is going to have the optimum opportunity to be extremely helpful and widely used.

On the Ground

After the meeting with staff members, Matt decided to proceed with a limited preplanned research initiative. Matt first needs to decide on a budget and has selected the specialized themed location events as his first project. Each location has a different clientele, and his staff needs to assess the demographic profile of each neighborhood in order to select the most lucrative sales approaches. Matt has questions as to how to go about finding out who lives in the nearby neighborhood. What do they like? What are their auto part preferences? Has this ever been done before by another auto parts store locally? Was it successful? How did they go about implementing it?

At the meeting, one of the staff members suggests they call an advertising agency and get an estimate for doing this demographic study. She assumes the agency has done this kind of work many times before; it could be completed fast and easily by a professional. Another employee suggests she visit to the local library and perform the research herself. She thinks this is very cost effective. Another staff member suggests going to the local university and hiring a student. What would you do? Matt is uncertain and does not want to spend money on "research" without some assurance that it will bring the desired result: i.e., selecting a clearly defined audience that will come to the location events and potentially buy specially priced products associated with the theme. He has a budget but knows it can be spent quickly if he is not careful. Does he hire a professional, a student, or do it in house? Either way, he still thinks going ahead is a good idea and knows he must be very involved in the process from beginning to end. Matt must now start thinking about promotion.

Chapter 5

WORKING FIRST WITH WHAT YOU HAVE

This chapter starts by looking at available methods for supplying inexpensive marketing research data. As previously stated, a lot of managers believe that they need to go out into the field for data when they are doing research, and this method can often be done with very little money. However, it is always more expensive for organizations to collect new information than it is to do an analysis of data that already exists and that is always there when management knows where it needs to look. In this section of the book, the goal is to let researchers on a shoestring budget know how to discover available information that has simply not been noticed or used by marketing managers who lack experience.

You can start by looking into untapped data you already have to find information that might relate to the decision that has to be made. However, there are often flaws in the conclusions about information from in-house experiments that do not receive sufficient analysis. This could be because the researcher does not have the savvy and experience needed to see deeply into the results of a certain study. It can also be a case of a researcher doubting the manager's comprehension ability when it comes to complex data and results. Excessive time pressure is often a frequent cause of flawed analysis.

USING EXISTING COMPANY INFORMATION

This can help in classifying information and organizing material. Additionally, it provides a checklist that outlines possible ways to use data that already exists. Two fundamental sources of data that already exist can be easily found by researchers working on a small budget.

> *You can start by looking into untapped data you already have to find information that might relate to the decision that has to be made.*

The first sources are records and documentation of events, actions, and outcomes in the past. These archives of data and records include an abundance of information ranging from invoices, financial records, correspondence, and more. Such archival sources can be divided again into internal records that the organization generates and external records that have been generated somewhere else.

The next source is made up of data that is not recorded at the moment, but that is easily observable. Watching the visitors of an organization's traffic flows, observing license plates in the parking lot to obtain a geographical profile of consumers, or placing individuals to interact with customers are all examples of this. There is some work involved with this type of information gathering, as the data must be sorted and stored in an easily accessible manner.

What both sources have in common is that they do not require direct questioning so that costs are kept low. Gathering information in a non-intrusive way has another big advantage as well: it may make the general quality of the research being done better. Studies have suggested that intrusive research can result in negative opinions being given by those studied. Final data may be distorted if the researcher asks questions that are too pointed and direct. This method may cause subjects to feel cautious and protective of their personal information. This is another way of saying that whatever is being measured can actually be changed by the very process of the measurement itself.

Inside Archival Sources

A majority of organizations already have a lot of data stored, and it can be divided into two categories. The first are those records that give some type of measurement, such as sales records, for instance. Transcribed data is another type of internal record data. It is kept in a non-numeric form. Often the numeric value must be determined and assigned before the data can be used. This kind of information might be complaints from customers, anecdotes about customer contacts, and reported visits to the sites of competitors. Just coding the information in each category is enough to offer valuable new things for a marketing manager to consider.

Inside Numerical Records

Many organizations gather and store a good deal of numerical information. This kind of data can provide great insight. You can get this kind of numerical information from sales reports, such as when publishers check newsstand sales to figure out which magazines and topics are most popular.

Because this kind of procedure hardly seemed satisfying, it was deemed wise and less biased to utilize an additional archive that of sales invoices to the separate outlets. While the database was undersized, the overall indications revealed that overly loading up of major retailers was a non-factor.

Single Transaction Records

Invoices from sales can provide insights into certain markets and can be open to many different kinds of analysis. If a majority of contacts result in transactions, their dates are helpful in calculating the frequency with which staff visit customers and the length of time that usually elapses between visits. Analyzing such transactions and what they bring in can show if the contact individuals are visiting at intervals that are proportionate to the returns one could expect. This analysis might show, in addition, if some customers who are favorites always get a visit even if there is no potential to make a sale.

To see whether some items or services are not satisfactory to customers, the company can also go through its refund receipts. In the same way, evaluating voided invoices is helpful in rating the kind of work that is being accomplished by individual employees. Sales invoices may be utilized as a check on other streams of information, for instance, to validate the report of a respondent on purchases that have been made. For example, a product distribution system would yield valuable information when studied by helping to verify purchase data reported during retail audits. When there are checks and balances in place, the researchers know they are working with the highest quality system available.

A great number of organizations have reports prepared by their employees, such as verbal comments from customers, gossip from trade shows, plus other important interactions in the marketplace. Evaluating the quality of the reports is useful to rate employee performance and to mark the trends that are emerging within the target market. It can be discovered if contact people are making the best use of their time by tracking the daily mileage according to the size of their territory. In addition, it will show whether the sales territories are not effective because they are too large or too small. When the business offers a service, different records like purchase orders can give a reliable sense of how frequently specific services are requested. The amount and length of Internet conversations or long-distance phone calls can be monitored as well to show the activity of employees and their pattern of contacting others.

Lots of internal data that is measurable does not show up in numerical form at first, which means somebody has to quantify it so that it becomes usable as research. Archival materials that fall into this slot are records of complaints, questions, and comments.

Records of Complaints

It is quite common for companies to get complaints or feedback from consumers, especially negative feedback from people who had a bad experience with the company or their products. Most companies do not take the time to analyze and store the information collected from these communications.

What is needed is a comparatively easy coding system which sets classifications for the following:

1. The associated organizational event or offering
2. The type of complaint and the circumstances surrounding it
3. The individual who initiated the contact
4. The place and date associated with the problem
5. The traits of both the individual making the complaint and the complaint itself

The data, although containing the possibility of rich information, is biased in a couple of ways. First, several studies found that individuals who voluntarily complain are not a real representation of every customer who may have reason to complain. If an individual wishes to be taken seriously by management when presenting a complaint, he or she must be able to express the complaint articulately and assertively. Generally speaking, people of higher social status and with greater education are capable of doing this. In general customers who may be more timid, lack assertiveness, or may be less educated will not speak up as often. For this reason, informal survey groups that consist of complaining customers are often biased toward certain interest groups and social classes. This unheard population can often be a large segment of your target audience, and not addressing these issues can be a large source of negative perceptions and feelings towards the organization and what it provides. That is why it is necessary to take time to find out what their complaints are by using an additional research strategy such as a small phone survey or a comment box.

The other cause of complaint data tilt is that the complaints obtained are not for certain representative of all forms of complaints. Minor issues are much less likely to be voiced as opposed to issues involving higher costs or levels of inconvenience. When the organization is obviously at fault, consumers are more likely to voice complaints as well. Silent issues, i.e., those not brought to the company's attention, can cause damage to the organization's reputation if they are not aggressively sought out, identified, and solved. Additionally, small problems lead to dissatisfied consumers who quietly stop patronizing the business without ever voicing their concerns.

While information regarding complaints is inherently biased, it may still be quite useful in pointing out the potential issues and obstacles an organization faces. It is particularly true if a firm is diligent in constantly analyzing such data. Differences in the amount and kinds of complaints that are seen as time goes on can either signify more problems or indicate that performance has improved.

While information regarding complaints is inherently biased, it may still be quite useful in pointing out the potential issues and obstacles an organization faces.

Even a minimal number of complaints could be sufficient to cue a manager to a potential problem that has to be seen to or it will injure a carefully structured marketing effort.

Lastly, analyzing complaints could have a secondary benefit as it helps in the evaluation of staff or partners that are fostering the mission of the organization. The field surveys are good tools for uncovering complaints so that companies can attend to the problems. A field survey can gain an independent assessment of partner and staff performance. This helps the company correct flaws before they cause problems.

Inquiries and Comments

There are forms of measurable communication that can be equally effective in helping with the management decision making process besides complaints, regardless of the fact that the preponderance of customer correspondence are complaints. Two wonderful instances of such communications are those that reflect product or service compliments or concerns and those that are sent between the employees of the company. Such communications, when they are analyzed correctly, are able to provide managers with insight into what their clients are thinking and can guide them into the strategies that will be best to implement in years to come. Traditional media outlets are a good example of this. Newspapers do an analysis of the letters to the editor that they get over the course of the year. That kind of analysis is able to show whatever shifts are occurring in the interests of those who read it.

Measurable, miscellaneous internal records: These include personal computer file data, appointment records, and calendars. Such information sources, when they are seen in combination with phone bills, records of expenses, and other data, can assist a manager in deciding whether personal time has been allocated for maximum efficiency. Computers know how to gather data on how users utilize the system, which software is most often engaged, and where the flow of traffic on the company website goes.

Information Centers

A method being adopted by comparatively large organizations to integrate and process internal data requires the operation of an information technology (IT) center. This serves the purpose of a consulting service to generate software and systems within the company server to allow shared access to information across the company database. An IT center is also there to show managers the types of databases they can find, and ways to utilize them. These people can teach managers various methods to go online to gather data and find resources that are external to the organization's typical sources. IT staff are frequently the ones whose job it is to set up the system and to select the hardware and software that the business will use. They usually also expend a number of hours consulting and coaching other users to assist them in evolving into more productive online researchers. IT systems are quite costly. If your research budget is small, the cost of your IT program should be split across several departments. It is also important to have the entire organization buy into the IT idea.

EXTERNAL SOURCES OF INFORMATION

You can separate external data, meaning it was not generated by the organization, into measurable collections of information. One example that is obvious is the use of data sources available at no cost or low cost online from major marketing research centers. Census information or journal articles might be included in such sources. Additional secondary information that can be measured is evidence of donor interest, facts about the organization in general, and the strategies of prospective partners. The data is available in raw numerical format.

Raw Data in Secondary Sources

There is a plethora of marketing information available for prices ranging from no cost, a one-time fee, or annual fees. Such data can be broken down into two main categories that have to do with whether it is raw data or information that has already gone through analysis after being broken down by other people. Although, when somebody else's raw data is used, it is important to know the possible biases that may reside in the data. Researcher and manager have to take into account these kinds of biases and be ready to adjust things as time goes on.

Secondary Sources Already Analyzed

There are times when low budget researchers do not have the sophistication, equipment, or time to invest in analyzing raw data produced by another. In such cases, outside data that is already been predigested might prove to be a good alternative. Studies and reports done by governmental agencies at various levels can be easily found on the Internet and in the library and make excellent resources for finding such data. They are often affordable and quite accurate.

These sources help accomplish a number of important research objectives. They can explain trends over time and reveal information about certain populations. Such data can assist in pinpointing future possibilities, establish quotas for things to be done later and provide resources that can help evaluate the business as well as the people who work for it.

Opportunities in foreign markets can be found in using governmental data sources. Gathering original information from other nations can generally be very expensive for U.S. researchers working on a tight budget. Government sources can provide data on populations and also on financial and social trends in many foreign nations. State organizations, financial institutions, chambers of commerce and local advertising firms create large amounts of data that entice businesses to move to their locations. Such data is often available to a researcher at no cost and may even be tailored to the needs of the study up to a point. Such data sources may in addition be supplemented by information given by foreign embassies as well as by Internet sources. Foreign market penetrating strategies are formed using all of the previously discussed information sources.

Syndicated Services

More useful secondary sources for marketers include assorted types of data which are supplied (for a fee) by syndicated services. Much of this can be gleaned from the typical Internet search engine such as Google, Bing, Yahoo, etc. Many search engines provide specific market research and have their own search capability. The information is often gleaned from research reports submitted by many sources.

The PRIZM system is an instance of predigested syndicated sources. Claritas Corporation gathers a lot of primary information for PRIZM on the over 42,000 zip code areas in America, while systems such as ACORN and MOSAIC offer similar services. MOSAIC also offers geo-clustering information in a few non-United States nations and industries. These are extremely valuable databases and are a staple for most market researchers.

It is necessary to be aware of the fact that since, in such cases, another person has gathered and preliminarily analyzed the data, the summaries might not completely match up with what the marketer is looking for. In addition, this means that already processed data will most likely cost more than the raw data. But no matter what, the manager on a tight budget can opt to be guided by these limitations and the possibility of more expense since he or she will not have the time nor the skill to do his or her own analysis.

You can find a great deal of external data online. This type of data is often available worldwide and in a number of different formats and indexes. These versatile and low-cost resources can allow a researcher to target specific locations, develop demographic market profiles - for the present as well as the future -as well as develop psychographic profiles, audience preferences, and media behavior patterns for consumers in the target market. Additionally, these resources allow a researcher to data mine for possible partnerships, find information on competitors - including locations and market saturation plans – and look for applicable economic and political trends. See Appendix 1 for a list of resources.

Decision makers need to take into account whether a search is going to be productive and provide useful information, regardless of the cost.

All you require to access this vast store of information is a computer and the passwords to every database. After a manager or researcher has enrolled in the system, a password will be given that will allow him or her to utilize the data that is received as needed.

Such services vary in price. Some will charge a sign-up fee, and some will charge for time spent connecting which will vary by when and how quickly the data is transmitted. In addition, you may have to spend more money for particular types of data. Decision makers need to take into account whether a search is going to be productive and provide useful information, regardless of the cost. Downloading and printing the data can also incur costs that need to be factored in to the total cost of the research. Because of this, a lot of online research professionals will copy the data onto an external drive of some sort or into cloud storage such as iDrive, Dropbox, or OneDrive, and then print it at another location.

A company might find it difficult to gather comprehensive and useful information when the person in charge is operating without input from others. However, if the media span being looked at is fairly slim, a manager can choose several print media samples as representative of the whole and name a staff member to scan them monthly or quarterly to discern the trends. If the major streams of media are taken care of, the manager needs to observe consistently and, even though the observations may be biased, note the ways in which significant social and economic indexes are changing. Commercial clipping services can perform this task as well for a low-cost fee.

Public Records

Records in the archives of public and semipublic institutions can serve as a great resource when trying to understand how outsiders see the organization and rate its performance. Articles both about the organization, including evaluations by rating agencies, as well as the organization's own submissions to websites, newspapers, magazines, or trade journals are important sources of publicity information. The organization's management will certainly be interested in comments about it and will be aware of that kind of publicity when they see it. When the details of such publicity are rated and recorded accurately, they can become the foundation for some valid research.

Gathering intelligence via other methods: Managers can learn a great deal about an organization's key players with analysis of repetitive activities. This technique is good for evaluating tactics and strategies with the passage of time. Just as critical are changes that happen once, though they can be more difficult to find.

Fortunately, there are several archives that can offer vital intelligence about what is happening within other organizations' management; among the online documents that serve this purpose are:

- Press releases for publicity purposes (such as those from the database PR Newswire)
- Lectures by people in the organization who aren't involved in marketing, such as attorneys and treasurers, who may not understand how what they say impacts a marketer.
- Pieces that have been created by people hired by an academic journal, the trade press, or popular magazines and newspapers.
- There may be ways to get an internal communication in an ethical manner. Such documents can be virtual mines of information on both prior policies and future plans.
- Biographical details of the key players whose past history might indicate what they will do in the future. This can be of particular value if an organization's or a political institution's leadership is changing.

In addition to the valuable online databases that are available to managers, one can also engage the use of other resources, such as:

- Get subscriptions to journals, trade magazines, conference minutes, and other periodicals that can provide valuable comments by those inside and outside the organization that are in the know.
- Get a subscription to a clipping service, which many Internet database vendors provide automatically.

- Services such as the Wall Street Transcript give you the highlights of corporate presentations for analysts and brokerage companies.
- Find somebody who can periodically check the search engines to see how the key players and your organization are referenced online.
- Have your employees to get in the habit of turning in all documentation related to customer visits, conferences attended and more as these could offer up important information about your own company as well as other important organizations and institutions at a relatively inexpensive cost.
- Buy shares of stock, and then you will have greater access to information about the history and future plans of the company.
- Mail out regular letters of inquiry to those who analyze industry or country data at the United States, The National Reference Center or the Departments of Commerce, Agriculture, or State.

SIFTING THROUGH THE DATA

Many methods can help when you want to collect and analyze what is communicated between key employees in the organization. To get evidence that is objectively recorded, it is necessary to do systematic content analysis. Advertising and many other data sources such as annual reports, publicity releases, direct mail messages, product packaging, and package inserts are all good candidates for this method.

But one should take certain steps when making determinations based on the resulting data, such as:

- Deciding which materials are to be analyzed has to be an objective, random process in order to make certain that the analyst's observation and internal bias does not overly influence the end result.

- A subset of these materials should have a trial analysis performed with rules set out to be utilized in cases that seem vague.
- Establish consistency among analysts and test the coding schemes' consistency and logic in an indirect way by assigning documents to multiple people to analyze.

No matter which sources the manager selects, it is necessary to have consistent streams of data generated and flowing as a matter of course into an affordable data bank. To do this, every document should be summarized in a report and filed, preferably electronically, so that it can be collated and reviewed if it is ever needed. As mentioned before, it is helpful to the marketing manager to know of pending changes before they actually happen.

On the Ground

Matt knows it is always more expensive to collect new information than it is to do an analysis of information that already exists. Is there useful market information about his customers and their preferences that is buried in the company records? Did the loyalty card program produce any usable data that generalizes the customer? Are there invoices, financial records, suggestion cards, or comments from some of his customers he has spoken with over the years? If so, where exactly is it and how do we go about finding it and turning it into useful market data? He has observed his customers for years. He thinks it is a good time to take a closer look at them and take notice of their buying habits. What do you think Matt could learn by observing? Are there "regulars?" How often do his customers come to stores? What time of day? How many cars are in the household? Are there families, singles, young, adults, seniors, etcetera?

He realizes there may be much to glean from simple observation and going through the receipts and looking more closely for trends and correlations that could prove valuable in explaining and understanding his customers. What about customers' complaints. What can he learn from those? He stops and realizes that he has not been to a competitor's auto parts store in almost five years. What is he missing out on by not keeping current with the latest trends? Matt is wondering if he could start "coding" information on his customers. He is thinking about 3 codes to start with: male/female, teen/young adult and adult/senior. As customers check out, the employee at the counter can add this into the receipt for future records. He can then correlate this with time of day and type of products bought.

Over the years Matt has not taken customer complaints too seriously. Last month a young man complained the store was not carrying a particular item. The employee responded that the store can't carry everything. After hearing that, Matt now is wondering if they ever came back. Maybe it is time to develop an effective method of finding out what customers think or want... a modern-day suggestion box of sorts. He does not want to be intrusive by asking his customers questions face to face or asking them to fill out a questionnaire. He is looking for some subtle unobtrusive alternatives. Can you think of some ideas for Matt to find out information from his customers without being pushy?

Chapter 6

COLLECTING INFORMATION

As previously detailed in the last chapter, archival information can be found just about everywhere a manager looks. The great manager is one that is not satisfied with getting insights only by chance, but instead wants to create opportunities for good, affordable research opportunities. The efficient and effective use of archival material rests on knowing where to look for the information as well as being committed to a systematic search to obtain the data.

> *The efficient and effective use of archival material rests on knowing where to look for the information as well as being committed to a systematic search to obtain the data.*

The same two principles can be applied to finding data from records that are not in writing, mainly observation of people, physical settings, and electronic environments.

In this chapter, we will concentrate on every step involved in the process of observation. To begin, researchers must come up with an opportunity to observe. Such events may be categorized as either observation that are one time or repeated and can further be separated into spontaneous or contrived occurrences. It is not sufficient to just establish the opportunity for observation; a good researcher also needs to know the proper way to observe. Therefore, various observational methods, as well as the procedures that make these methods helpful and effective, are addressed.

When you are seeking high quality research that is also affordable, you cannot do better than using systematic observation. These observations symbolize available goods that professionals currently utilize on a daily basis. There are a few things researchers and managers can do to gain information about their competitors and their organizations, as well as their target market: order service from the competitor, visit the competitors' establishments, evaluate the competitors' advertising, and observe customers' reactions. It is also a good idea for supervisors to look for effective results using innovative methods. This could mean using the first names of clients for a time to see what effect that has on their buying, redoing their display cases, or rearranging the room to see the effect it has on traffic. Many marketers are already doing this type of free research, although the majority of it is neither systematic nor goal-oriented. All too frequently, marketers regard casual observations as if they were nonessential, as opposed to making an effort to be systematic and open-minded all through the process. That takes some effort, as it is required that there be systems in place to record the data, as well as some type of preplanning. In addition, this necessitates that those who observe are trained to be neutral and thorough in their observations.

To reiterate, you can use observations and archival information once or as part of continuing projects. Situational, short-term research is the most-common starting point for one-time observation. One example of this is the situation in which managers looking into company relocation observe local demographics in order to make predictions. A manager in this situation might observe local income levels, typical traffic volumes, types and ages of vehicles in the area, and so on.

In both single and ongoing circumstances, observations are frequently composed of one or a combination of these activities: counting, measuring, or pattern seeking. These can be done in a very subtle manner or as part of the direct process of observation. Observations can be conducted in a variety of ways ranging from electronic equipment to direct observation by researchers. The goal of counting is to determine market demand or the efficacy of marketing techniques. This research is quantifying objects, individuals, and behaviors that apply to the desired information.

Counting can frequently be the one thing a manager can do to assess what effects the competition's actions or various surprising events can have. For instance, vacant parking lot spaces may imply the impacts of a competitor's sale or of an oncoming ice storm. A good thing about counting is that even untrained researchers can do it. Managers need not squander their expensive time conducting simple research that could be done by temporary employees hired for that purpose. You will need to have clear instructions, but the overall costs are low and the information gained can be very valuable.

MEASUREMENT

Observation is most helpful when it contains some kind of measurement instead of just counting individuals, things, or actions. It can end up especially helpful when measuring the environmental features of concern which are left behind. Researchers who look for such physical traces function in a way as archaeologists of contemporary living.

Mechanical or Electronic Observation

An apparent issue with a simple method such as counting might be human error. Mistakes in recording information can still occur when your otherwise highly competent staff is overstressed and/or overtired. These errors do not have to kill the project, though, if you take time to have a debriefing following a research session or do a comparison of results from different researchers so that you can detect systematic failings.

When human researchers are involved, other issues may come up as well. They might only want to have hours in the late evening or early morning, meaning that a lot of environments will not get researched. A bigger issue is if when having a human observer becomes so intrusive or distracting to the subjects that it causes a problem. Customers may feel discouraged from looking at products or looking into services if they see a researcher hanging around a certain display or hovering in the door with a mechanical counter or clipboard. Nonetheless, biases can be surpassed if the biases are somewhat alike between observations. Data will always have biases, but when you keep this fact in mind, you will be better equipped to minimize them.

An affordable substitute to minimize the possibility of human error or bias is found by using observation strategies that are electronic or mechanical in nature. This type of research is used by major commercial research services and is used quite frequently. Some examples might include the Nielsen television ratings, garnered by observation of the viewing habits of sample households, and hidden cameras that capture the reactions of consumers to advertising materials.

> *Data will always have biases, but when you keep this fact in mind, you will be better equipped to minimize them.*

Within the field of packaged goods, electronic scanning is an important development with regard to market research. This allows the researcher to capture the purchases of sample households. If an item has a barcode, it can be electronically measured. Keep in mind however, that it takes a certain amount of money and sophistication to be able to take advantage of this technology.

One can also, less expensively, use mechanical car counting. This counts cars by using a rubber hose placed across the street. Such counters can be very helpful to monitor things, even though mistakes can happen (like trucks with three-axles or people that keep going back and forth).

Visual counting devices can be utilized. This will count each time a person passes through the beam of light.

- Cameras that work digitally are useful. Much information can be observed when you look at photos. To use an auto parts store as an example, a marketing manager could photograph the viewers of another performance to get a sense of the characteristics of the audience, such as age. When used in repetition, this sort of technique is helpful in measuring the popularity of a variety of performers and performances in different venues.
- Video recording equipment can be used for observation. Visual data such as clothing types and gender allocation of the customer base as well as other information can be gathered using recorded images. In addition, they may show patterns of movement, such as how people who go to the store might begin finding what they need. A camera will show you how the employees approach clients, the length of time the latter remain on the property, how they circulate through the store and other important details.
- Software for the computer is useful for tracking a customer's patterns on the Internet through the website, and note which items he or she searches, and the amount of time spent on one specific page.
- Use natural observation to identify patterns. When mechanical or electronic devices are used for measurement, the human scale of identifying certain patterns is neglected. An anthropologist's specialty will be looking for physical traces, then synthesizing what they have found and reading any patterns that show up.

If you are trying to stay below budget, it is wise to do assessments of crucial events in a variety of ways. Many of the strategies this book outline advocate methodology compromises so as to keep things affordable. That means the information gleaned from an inexpensive study has to always be examined with a critical eye and knowledge that this data could be biased or not thorough because of budget issues. Getting similar results using different research techniques means that the researcher can be confident that their results are accurate.

Observations and research findings need to be both systematic and purposeful if they are to be trusted by management and considered valid. The goal of your research design should be to gather a sample that reflects your targeted audience and intended goals.

To attain this result, two crucial steps need to be taken. First, there needs to be the development of a sampling procedure so that every prospective observation has the same chance to be recorded and used. Secondly, a researcher must stay as neutral and unattached as possible so that no one has to question that there has been any internal bias.

Getting similar results using different research techniques means that the researcher can be confident that their results are accurate.

Observation is one way to gather information, similar to asking for responses on a questionnaire. However, many researchers who are good about carefully designing a plan prior to sending interviewers out will still be too offhanded when it comes to sending people out in the field. There are two ways to record observations at a variety of locations. You can either record an equal number of observations at each location, or you can record a proportion of relevant observations that represent the outcomes expected at each location. In each instance, the researcher has to first decide the number of potential observations that can be done at each site so that there is a base line from which to make comparisons with the data that is actually collected. Researchers need to have some guidelines for observing, even when the spots and the times for these will be randomly chosen. Systematic sampling is the simplest thing to do, which means a pre-set observation pattern is followed, such as noticing every sixth individual who passes on the south side of a building's entrance.

Regardless of the procedure, the hope is that the observer will come away with a firm rule and will follow a recording and observation pattern that is measurable and consistent rather than simply viewing things that are easy or interesting to look at.

While some researchers are methodical and careful in their studies, others work in ways that are poorly thought out and poorly documented.

The suggestions that follow will help make certain that the highest quality research occurs:

1. Find those to observe who, according to statistics, are apt to be neutral and to pay attention to the task.
2. Test these individuals on observational abilities so that you weed out the prospects that are not as capable.
3. Create specific directions and instructions outlining the "what" and the "how." Make this crystal clear - precisely and specifically what to observe and how to accomplish it.
4. The observers should practice as much as possible prior to starting the actual process of conducting the survey and observation.

Inexpensive Experiments

Managers should be skeptical of the use of past successes as predictions for what will work in the future. What will work in the future, not the past, is what is desired. A highly cost-effective way of determining this, both financially and in terms of time expended, is to try out various research approaches with limited populations. With this sort of immediate experimentation, managers are able to determine whether implementing one tactic will cause a specific result or not. This helps them predict circumstances that may exist in future decisions and projects.

Managers can be shown that experiments will provide the following advantages to them and to the jobs they are responsible for:

- They give the researcher the ability to control the process so that it better falls in line with the strategic options management has set and helps to facilitate decisions.
- These experiments allow the one doing the research to control a great deal of the external factors that might be at odds with the process of long term research.

- These can aid in proving cause and effect by indicating that, when all else was kept constant, the result X must have arisen from A.
- They make the process of observing and researching quicker and more efficient than any other approach.

A majority of the large marketers who work in the private sector will perform experiments as a matter of course. When developing new products and services, test marketing, which is actually experimenting in the real world, is a very commonly used technique. Possible demand for products, responses to various advertising campaigns, or finding out how desirable a specific change in buildings or signs might be assessed with a market test.

Most managers do not think that an experiment is an affordable type of research to complete. However, it may work quite well and often provides a very affordable research strategy. Frequently, when managers are under pressure to come up with results without monetary aid, they tend to be as careful as possible. That way of doing things tends to keep the experimentation to a minimum. Managers may decide that it is not worth the time or trouble to put forth the effort – this is not ideal. This is faulty reasoning on many levels, not the least of which is the assumption that the manager was able to identify the best choice without research. Nonetheless, if the experiment's expenses can be kept down, that may be a worthwhile investment of time and money when it raises the probability of finding out which is really the best choice.

If a manager is sophisticated, he or she will think about the long-term and its potential in a strategic manner. This perspective helps managers accept that, in the short term, there will be some experimentation failures that will ultimately lead to success. Managerial experimentation turns into a system that builds intelligence and understanding within the business.

Designing Studies

There are many different studies that a marketer can pursue. What experiments ultimately try to do is to take a new approach and see, following some key experiment rules, what affect this new way of doing things will have on the desired result. All of the marketing steps can be examined as to their current effectiveness and possibilities for improvement. There can be trials of new products and services, readjustment of prices, promotion of benefits, or hours of operation changed. When experiments are implemented, both large and small issues can be addressed.

Experimentation can happen in the real world or in a lab. Real world research is the most easily applicable form of research; however, it is also the most influenced by outside factors that are not always easily identified and overcome. In a lab setting, external factors may be constant, but what we get in terms of control may be lost when the process naturally meets reality later on. The results of an experiment can be organized in terms of ideas, actions, or a combination of both. Cognitive data includes measuring awareness, how different communications are perceived, what is preferred, attitudes about patronizing a place in the future, and possible word of mouth referrals. Measurements of behavior could be responses from customers and activities of the staff as well as of prospective and existing partners.

The results of an experiment can be organized in terms of ideas, actions, or a combination of both.

There are three parts an experiment needs to possess in order to yield data that will help management in its role. First, you need to assign various experimental treatments, such as various types of communication, randomly to different groups of people - that is, populations, individuals, or geographic areas. Next, the design of the experiment should be developed so that there isn't anything else that could have caused the results that were observed. Third, the outcome of the experiment needs to be able to be projected into a future marketing scenario the organization will face, and it needs to be clearly applicable to a real-life situation.

TYPES OF EXPERIMENTS

Good experiments come in many forms and may be complex; this is the reason why the book you are reading concentrates mostly on relatively simple procedures for experiments. We will look at the two most common and simplest experiments first, then address some more in depth and involved procedures for those whose decision-making process is, by necessity, more complex.

After Measure with Control

This is the simplest experiment in both design and administration. That means the researcher needs to assign people to at least two groups randomly, with one being a control group and the other receiving a particular treatment. After that, the results of every treatment can be measured in comparison with the control group that has not been treated. That takes away whatever systematic bias might exist between groups, but from time to time, random differences can turn up.

Before and After Measures with Control

A researcher must always entertain the idea that there are other explanations for effects besides the treatment. One possibility is that there were differences present in the sample populations before the study was completed, and in reality, the treatment did not have any effect. That can happen even if there has been random assignment of groups.

A majority of studies that involve changes in cognition are quite easily contaminated in the pre-measure phase. It is preferable to have after-only measures in cases like that. For researchers, pre-measure is a very important component of research. If there is no pre-measure or inaccurate pre-measure, it can skew results. On the whole, the higher the number of cases being attached to each condition, the more relaxed the researcher can pay attention to previous differences among groups. Thus, the researcher can safely select the after-only method. If researchers are just looking at variations in treatment, it is possible to use contaminating pre-measures. Some believe that the use of pre-measure causes an increase in post measures and does not increase the end effects of any specific measure. In such instances, it is assumed that all the groups have a bias and that the researcher can do a comparison of the biased treatment differences and also the biased control group differences.

Additional sources of bias may be present even though the researcher has made the safe assumption that there have been none in the pre-measure stage. Test subjects often know what is happening, and as a result, their behavior changes and is not normal for the situation.

Experimental Designs That Are Complex

We have several choices open to us when we want to conduct complex experiments through direct mail at an affordable price. Many organizations put in a lot of time and effort to send out mailings, print brochures, send out press releases, put out advocacy letters, solicit volunteers, and more, just to try to get a response. Having said that, it would still be of great value to find out how to get a greater response, particularly positive feedback.

It would be natural to go with experimentation here since there are many reasons why direct mail is so often used:

- It is simple enough to randomly assign subjects for the experiment.
- Because many subjects can be assigned to every group, there is almost no need to have a pre-measure.
- It makes it simple to track the responses that come from particular groups.
- Conditions for treatment can be carefully managed.
- Mailings are private so it is unlikely that the competition will find out about the experiment.

- The validity of external data is high because the results of a mailing experiment will usually be used by the marketer over time.
- Recipients on a mailing list probably won't realize they are participating in an experiment, so any potential bias is limited.
- When you have a large sample base you can have many complete interaction assessments with no compromise of accuracy.

Direct mail programs are a great way for any researcher to do a low-cost campaign, and email campaigns will lower the costs even more.

Lab Experiments

In spite of the issues they present, lab experiments are often quite valuable as substitutes for field experiments. These can be performed in college classrooms, kiosks at shopping malls, hotel rooms, or even at work. The benefit of a lab study is that there can be tight control over many factors with those that are unnecessary completely eliminated in most cases. That is why lab experiments involving touch, taste, and smell are very popular. Additionally, service concept tests, new product tests, prices studies, and communications studies that use these techniques are well received. The laboratory provides the opportunity to use such devices that could not be used out in the field, for example, electronic measurement tools.

Two advantages to experiments in a lab are their affordability and their ability to be done rapidly. That means that easy lab experiments are frequently a great initial step when you want to test new concepts or strategies.

Experiments that seem to be conducted with ease: When the manager considers the approaches possible in experimental design, a good understanding of both the potential problems and benefits of the chosen techniques is desirable.

When certain conditions exist, doing the experiment should be pretty easy, such as when the pre-measures are already in existence. If the samples have to be small because of financial issues, information about past revenues or reviews from customers can be utilized in order to check for possible bias.

- The recording of pre-measures, where no pre-measure exists, may still be utilized without affecting the study and still decreasing possible negative pre-measure effects.
- Frequently, the time span between a procedure and its measurement is so slim that there is no external environmental effect, and this lessens the need to monitor such possible contaminating elements.
- If the population is very similar to each other, a pre-measure may not be required when serious thought is given to randomization.
- If there are worries that only one or two measures of experimental outcomes might produce biased results, multiple measures may be used to prevent individual biases from canceling one another out.
- With more experience on the part of the researcher, it is frequent that a strong estimate can be made regarding potential biasing effects.

If the opportunity presents itself, you can ask the subjects of the studies if they considered any features of the study design to have had an influence on their results. That is known as debriefing, which is routinely done in many different kinds of experiments that involve human subjects. Ethical considerations mean that subjects need to be told of their rights not to participate; in addition, they should be informed after the debriefing of exactly what the study was supposed to accomplish and who the sponsor was.

Make sure that staff members are not putting bias into what they find, even though they may not intend to.

In the final analysis: Here are some of the key points we should reiterate before ending our discussion of the topic of experimental research methods. First, be certain that the experiment has been created in such a way that it will be helpful to management in making decisions. Do not just conduct research for its own sake.

- Decide ahead of time that you will measure the experiment's results in different ways to make certain that the perceived effects actually occurred and that oddities and biases do not hide something crucial or hint at something that isn't. In addition, it is vital to make sure that the sample population has been randomized.
- When doing field research, be sure to check for possible outside influences.
- Do not rush to judgment as to the outcome without letting sufficient time elapse after treatment has occurred.
- Think about the possibility of utilizing many different treatments as you go through the experiment.
- Make sure that staff members are not putting bias into what they find, even though they may not intend to.
- When possible, be sure to have the subjects, including those on staff, debriefed following the study to find out if there were biases.
- When the experiment is finished, notice what you learned in order to have a relevant starting point for the next set of experiments. This allows the researcher to increase efficiency for future experiments, thus controlling costs even more effectively, as well as providing data for management to base marketing strategy decisions on.

On the Ground

Matt decides to be more proactive in taking notice of his customers and competitors in hopes of noticing patterns and trends resulting in providing more value to his customers. The first thing he is going to do is go to a competitor in the next town with his family and take note of everything he can-from the parking lot to the restrooms to the product offerings to any advertisements he can see. He is going to do this every two months for a while. While he is there he is going to see what kind of customers are there, customer demographics. How friendly is the staff? How knowledgeable is the staff? What kind of cars are in the parking lot? How many are there? Are they expensive? Is the lot full? How does that compare with his customers? Why are they coming here and not to his store?

Matt wonders if he can "interview" some of his customers. He wants to make sure he can get a representative sample of each market segment without having to interview every single customer who walks in. He also wants to select an employee who will be diligent in the process and who makes a good appearance. He is skeptical about using Joe who has a couple of noticeable tattoos. He is concerned his customers may be put off and not answer honestly. He also has to decide what questions to ask. What would you suggest he do first?

He is also considering conducting a focus group but knows they are expensive and is not sure if his budget will allow him to experiment with this kind of intensive study. He has participated in a focus group one time with an investment club and felt he was not completely transparent with his answers. He knew he was being studied and tried to speculate on the reasons particular questions were being asked. Because of that he was inclined to keep vital information to himself because he felt uncertain about the motivations driving the questions. He does not want that to happen in this research study. What do you think he should do?

Chapter 7

BASIC SURVEYS

Researchers working with tight economic constraints have to expand their knowledge base and come to realize that they have potential research methodologies available to them besides questionnaires and surveys. The last chapter goes over experimentation; the chapters prior to that discuss two other very important choices of surveys: archives and observation. Even though they still have value in that they are very inexpensive options, these techniques are sometimes less practical since they do not easily lend themselves to cause and effect assessments. Even with their issues, such strategies will frequently offer managers the edge they need to make decisions that will have them consistently outperforming the competition.

Scrutinizing those options may be beneficial to the research process as carrying out successful surveys can be expensive and problematic. Surveys can be complex for a couple of reasons: First, they usually need a representative sampling, which can be difficult to get. Secondly, conducting a survey means that questions need to be asked, which have their own set of issues attached. There is always some intrusion involved in asking questions, as the participants understand they are being studied and so will often try to speculate on the reason a particular question is being asked. That can result in either of two different effects. Firstly, test subjects may be inclined to keep vital data to themselves or to report it in a deceptive manner because they feel uncertain about the motivations driving the company.

> *One of the most favored words used when studying retail and service establishments through questions is "convenience."*

The awareness of the respondent also comes into play when they make an estimate of the sort of information the researcher is looking for and begin to modify their answers in order to attempt satisfy them. Respondents can be naturally inclined to provide exaggerated positive responses to the subject under discussion, especially if they believe that doing so will in some way please the researcher or satisfy his or her expectations. Even when people are not conscious of it, we all try to have influence over the ways in which we are perceived. Thus, it is almost certain that participants will be tempted to give answers that make them feel better about themselves.

Language is used when questions are asked, and words can be interpreted in a variety of manners. One of the most favored words used when studying retail and service establishments through questions is "convenience."

Sadly, such problems are unavoidable within this type research. Among the biggest of the problems is when the researchers are not certain that they have stamped out potential biases. Management requires valid research results as a basis to make their decisions. Conducting surveys and asking questions is usually crucial for a particular management issue. Such strategies have to be used by researchers in a lot of different situations, but they must always bear in mind that whatever results are obtained need to be of help to the management team.

SURVEY DESIGN

There are three overarching themes in the design of every survey:

1. *How* will the questions be asked?
2. *What* questions need to be asked?
3. *Who* is answering the questions?

Additionally, precise questions that the researcher should include are:

1. Does he or she want respondents to have the opportunity and time to confer with peers prior to delivering an answer?
2. Is it possible for the answers to be streamlined down to several easy choices?
3. Do these questions require that the respondent be given an explanation?
4. Does it seem that the answers given by the respondent will need clarification?

Methods of Asking Questions

Today, researchers can choose one or more of the many questioning approaches made possible through technology. Such strategies will vary based on the amount of interaction between the asker and the responder. Use of Internet, telephone, and in-person interviews are all candidates, but there are additional options. The interview process may include individuals or groups in public or private settings, by prerecorded telephone or computer. There are situations in which it might be appropriate to use a combination of techniques. For instance, a study could begin with an in-person interview which is supplemented by a mail-in questionnaire left for the respondent to fill out at his or her leisure with detailed information like personal preferences, socioeconomic figures, and past buying decisions.

Mail Surveys

The modest budgets at the disposal of many researchers naturally incline them towards doing mail studies; often because they believe they cannot afford anything more. Generating a mailing list is not usually a challenge, since pre-developed lists are available for purchase, and some list sellers also offer mailing labels and can even perform the entire mailing project themselves. Even if they do not have a prepared list, a lot of researchers think they can create one themselves by utilizing their own or existing databases (i.e., ReferenceUSA). Clerical help will be able to stuff envelopes without the project incurring more costs, and the price of sending the questionnaires can be kept low with a postage meter or by using bulk rates. Since business reply envelopes are used to returned responses, you only have to pay for postage for questionnaires that are actually returned.

There are two subtypes of those interested in the topic: individuals excited about the topic and those who see an opportunity to air grievances and/or dissatisfaction with the topic.

Because of such low costs, a lot of researchers make the decision to jump in. A researcher may only get from ten to fifteen percent of responses back if this is a normal set of questionnaires that has been sent out to a random but relatively interested set of potential participants. There could still be a large amount of those responding, depending upon the number that was first sent out. This is the place where the researcher should not worry about the respondents, but rather should be concerned about the non-respondents. As a mall study often has low a response rate, the nature of the non-response bias is commonly unknown. It is not bad if there is no response, but the researcher can be assisted if he or she knows why someone has chosen not to answer. Sometimes the problem is a refusal to reply, the survey taker is not home, distracted, or an erroneous house or telephone number has been used. The result is lack of feedback. If the interviews were set for different weekday and weekend times and several attempts at follow up were made, it is more probable that a non-response was a chance happening that did not mean those people were different from those who did answer.

However, with research done through the mail that hardly ever happens. People who receive a letter that requests they answer a set number of questions will naturally feel imposed upon. The same can be said for phone interviews. Whether in personal or phone interviews, the well-trained interviewer with skill and personality can help get past these initial negative feelings. It is easier, however, for a prospective respondent to throw a mailed questionnaire into the trash immediately upon receipt or when it is sitting on the desk or kitchen counter at home. People who did not respond like this are apt to differ in one of two significant ways. One set of responders will show an inherent interest in the subject being studied. The next group wants to assist the researcher, being a helpful type of person or swayed momentarily by the way the study's cover letter has convinced them. There are two subtypes of those interested in the topic: individuals excited about the topic and those who see an opportunity to air grievances and/or dissatisfaction with the topic.

What may we understand about the ten to fifteen percent of individuals who reply to the usual mail survey? It means they will usually differ a lot from those who do not respond. Sadly, a lot of researchers do not have the patience to analyze these possible differences because they either do not see the problem, do not know how to deal with it, or think they are short of time or money.

Nevertheless, there are things that can be done by a manager or researcher to help improve rates of response as well as to find out more about non-response bias, even if these things might be expensive. Even if the rates of non-response have been processed, questionnaires sent through the mail have a lot of other, frequently more problematic, flaws. For instance, it is quite possible that another person besides the intended respondent would be filling out the questionnaire. One spouse might request that the other one do the responding. Executives may have a subordinate take care of this task. A physician could request that a nurse respond to the questions. Any of these circumstances could cause the findings to be seriously distorted. The survey taker may have too much time to think about their responses and change their first thoughts. The ability to get honest answers is compromised, and they will change their answer to what they believe will make the consensus taker happy.

There still remains some circumstances in which mail surveys could be a great option: First, when a respondent would need a lot of time to find the answers the questionnaire requires. That could involve a consultation with another person. For instance, if the researcher wanted to know if anybody in the home had purchased an item, used a service, or done something new, then he or she would have to allow time to consult with other people. That would often not be a practical option when doing a phone or in-person interview.

Second, in many circumstances, you must let the respondent have sufficient time to give a thoughtful answer. That occurs when the questions are complex or need to be thought about deeply to give an effective answer.

A Likert type, or categorical questionnaire (1 to 5, mostly agree, mostly disagree) is most likely the only format that busy people would take the time from their schedule to answer. Nonetheless, if the questionnaire is long, people will be less likely to spend time on it.

Even when this happens, a mail study should only be an option if the following things are in place.

- It does not have a detrimental effect on the research if someone other than the addressee answers the questionnaire.
- You can get a mailing list or similar sampling process that represents the population you are most interested in.
- There can be a careful assessment of what the non-response bias really means.
- The people responding to the survey can read and have a mailing address.
- It is extremely likely that a large portion of those responding would be interested in the subject and so therefore participate.

There are a couple of circumstances under which you can utilize a mail survey that is biased. One is when the researcher is unconcerned regarding the non-response group. It would apply at any time when it is not critical to project an outcome. This is true in some circumstances such as when a researcher wants to find out if a product, service, ad, or instructions have any problems. Another rationale for a biased study is to employ it for exploratory purposes. A common situation where this might occur is when a company is building up hypotheses to use in a larger study later, testing new research materials or gathering fresh ideas for advertising purposes.

After having decided to do a study by mail, many fundamental techniques need to be used. The first is that a cover letter that includes a motivational element must be written. An ideal cover letter must have several goals: It must have a positive approach; it must explain the reasons that the study is being conducted (and ideally show that participating is in the respondent's best interest); it must guarantee privacy; and it should present a call for assistance, thus encouraging greater response by reminding respondents that they are members of a select group with vital information to share. There are some other techniques to increase the value of a study by mail:

- Make use of color and appropriate graphics to make your attractive, professional looking cover letter and questionnaire stand out.
- The letter should be addressed to a particular person.
- When possible, use professional letterhead for motivational purposes. The letter should do so if the sponsor of the study can be identified and if that awareness would potentially motivate respondents.
- Keep the questionnaire as short as you can to make sure the reader is able to follow and make sense of the questions. A self-addressed stamped return envelope or email address should accompany the survey. If there are ample funds in the budget, follow up visits or phone calls can be made to improve the rates of response. It will raise the total amount of responses as well as their speed and

quality when the researchers can give the participants advance notice that the survey is on its way.
- If possible, give a reward or perk to those who respond. It increases how many responses you get, how fast you get them, and the quality of the response.

A crucial piece of online research includes who is being contacted and who has decided to respond.

Many professional researchers advise dropping off and picking up the surveys personally instead of mailing them. They think this strategy works especially for long surveys where there needs to be a lot of effort put into motivation and explanation. Studies have shown that there may be rates of response of as much as eighty percent. Although reaching this level of participation does require paying employees to get the questionnaires to and from respondents, the amount of training and compensation required are minimal. The cost of each returned questionnaire was not found to be any different from the traditional questionnaire sent through the mail. Not only can the questionnaire deliverers save time by skipping over potential respondents who are clearly outside the area of interest, they can also gather basic observational data (like their neighborhood, housing, age, and sex) to provide a wider range of information.

Electronic Surveys

The Internet is a great resource when you want to make contact with possible participants. Internet survey companies believe that at least one third of the world's population is online and more than forty five percent of them lived in the U.S. and Canada. An online survey lets a researcher or manager list complex questions that are customized to each particular respondent. On the Internet, individual respondents can see a variety of stimuli, for example, TV commercials, print ads, and so forth – the can subsequently provide their opinions and responses. This gives the Internet an advantage over other survey methods. Such research is somewhat difficult to design, but there are several organizations that are ready to assist with this and implement online research projects.

A crucial piece of online research includes who is being contacted (the sample) and who has decided to respond (the respondent). Those who use the Internet do not really represent an entire country's population, particularly when it is a developing country, new to the Internet resources. Internet users are stereotypically young, better educated, and on the higher end of the economic spectrum. Lastly, a participant could make believe he or she is somebody of a totally different demographic without the researcher knowing, which means it is impossible to control who the respondents really are. Maybe the most helpful thing about online research tools is that they can be designed to provide managers with the impressions and insights they need to make decisions.

Using social media platforms on the Internet can provide the researcher with accurate and timely information and has the potential to tap millions of people for data. More about this is found in the chapter on leveraging social media for marketing research.

The ease with which researchers can gather information on respondents' behavior lets them relay a very clear description of the bias towards non-responsiveness to researchers. That means the study it not done nationally but rather in a more specific geographical spot. Particularly useful in organizational or office studies, this technique is easy to locate but is busy enough so that they would not ordinarily agree to a personal interview.

Telephone

In many first world nations, phone interviewing is getting to be the preferred method particularly if a researcher has to interact with participants in order to obtain a sample that can be projected across a few different media. The low cost of this method makes it one of the more popular types of research. There are distinctive benefits to interviews conducted by phone that other methods lack, including the following:

There is enough of a personal connection to achieve the same level of familiarity as in a face-to-face conversation, yet the respondent cannot form an impression of the interviewer's appearance, mannerisms and style, and this reduces one significant source of potential bias effects.

Respondents answering questions of a personal nature will be less likely to become embarrassed and withhold information in a phone interview, since they can speak to the interviewer without watching their reactions or seeing them record the responses. Multiple callbacks and the setting of appointments lets interviewers seek the particular people they need. Because phone interviews often take place in one location, a supervisor is able to easily check on the work being done through informed eavesdropping so as to have greater quality control and uniformity of technique.

Notwithstanding those numerous advantages, telephone interviewing suffers from three impactful shortcomings:

1. Motivation and rapport are far more difficult on the phone than when in person since it is easier to hang up on someone than to shut the door in his or her face.
2. Many issues cannot be tackled in a phone interview that can be addressed in person. You cannot use visuals or even certain measurement assists, like scales or cue cards.
3. Not only are some home telephone numbers (especially in large communities) unlisted, but that people are getting rid of land lines all together, switching to mobile phones which are more difficult to call without certain software programs).Telephone directories, traditional or electronic are not a good sampling frame for interviewing in most major centers. Digital Trend magazine indicated that while about 47 percent of the 21,517 households polled only use cellphones, roughly 41 percent still have both landlines and mobile phones. About 8 percent of those in the

survey don't have cells at all, and around 3 percent are completely phoneless.

If a telephone is used in the sampling framework, there are then specific processes to follow when selecting the number to contact. Because of this, implementing a fluctuation of arbitrary numbers or adding one when dialing is usually promoted for the above-mentioned individuals who have the intention of using various specimens of telephone numbers. Such an approach means initially doing a random selection from a directory to make certain that the one doing the research is making use of number blocks that the phone company has already released. Right here, the last one or two digits in the listing number are substituted with other randomly chosen numbers.

Or the researcher could just add a one to the last digit in the number that's been chosen. Compared to sticking strictly with the numbers appearing in the directory, approaches such as these introduce minimal bias, although they can still overlook large groups of numbers introduced after the directory's last publication date. The random digit dialing approach has its drawbacks as well. It may make things more expensive, if for instance, the numbers that were selected at random wind up being fax lines or organizations that are not eligible. This is generally an accepted cost of business though. If the volume of individuals to contact is high, more sophisticated electronic approaches are available.

There are new programs referred to as 'robo-callers.' These automated software packages can call your landline or mobile phone with greater speed and efficiency. In addition, there are added features such as making the call appear that it is from the same area code, making it more likely that you will answer the phone.

Interviewing Face-to-Face

There are many reasons why one-on-one interviews are excellent for this sort of study. Once respondents are contacted, they typically are very motivated to cooperate with the study. When you take care in selecting the interviewers, such as by making their traits similar to those they will be interviewing and by offering motivational instructions, there will likely be a low rate of refusal. Thus, the stimuli that can be shown to or handled by respondents in particular sequences is very important in instances where the researcher wishes to assess responses to promotion materials such as advertisements or brochures, or where a product or package needs to be tasted, sniffed, or otherwise inspected. Contacting respondents via computer, mail, or self-reporting simply does not provide the same level of feedback provided by meeting them in person or interviewing them over the phone. This allows the respondent to give more elaborate answers or to get more help on questions that are not immediately understood.

In addition, the interviewer has the chance to put in observational measurements besides traditional questioning. For instance, when a collection of advertisements is shown, the interviewer can approximate the time duration spent by the respondent on every stimulus. Facial expressions and other non-verbal communication can be examined in addition to appearance and environment of their home or office. Without directly asking a respondent for data, there are details that can be observed and recorded, such as: sex, race, age, and social class.

The impression of the interviewer may trigger the respondent to consciously or sub-consciously adjust the given answers.

These benefits, however, are contrasted by drawbacks equally as important and problematic. In truth, when the correspondent appears in person for an interview, predispositions of the interviewer can be anticipated. First, the way the interviewer looks, acts, smells, dresses, or speaks could have a particular influence on a respondent. The impression of the interviewer may trigger the respondent to consciously or sub-consciously adjust the given answers. Also, the mere presence of another individual may cause the respondent to distort responses by trying to make an impression on the interviewer or to omit a fact that could potentially be embarrassing. That type of research frequently gets quite expensive. Phone calls and mail can go to any place in the nation and most places around the globe rapidly and very efficiently. It might be too costly and time consuming to have one on one interviews and may result in inefficient use of resources.

Many low-cost sampling methods could be considered once the decision is made to proceed with personal interviews.

When a researcher wants to interview on a tight budget, each possible participant needs to have a recognized probability for being selected. There are two approaches generally utilized.

Focus Groups

Many survey designs that are inexpensive will provide results that are very statistically relevant. Using focus groups is one very common, affordable strategy for doing face-to-face interviews. When choosing this method, up to a dozen people may come together to discuss the research topic.

It is impossible to project the results of focus groups, (which are also qualitative), and they are usually engaged for these tasks:

- Hypothesis generation
- Gathering data for use in questionnaire design
- Adding to an exchange category's background data
- Finding consumer ideas for new communications, services, or products
- Clarifying results of earlier studies
- Testing reactions to new lines of communication, organizational restructuring, products or other shifts in promotion strategy.

There are a greater number of intelligent thoughts and perspectives in a group than would be offered with a single interview or what the researcher may consider on his or her own.

There are significant advantages to using focus groups. There is a good amount of group interaction that focus groups offer and are a chief draw for researchers. They also provide the benefit of increased cost-efficiency.

If using a focus group was not in the budget, many researchers would use it due to synergism. Since each participant can adapt, respond, or critique the comments of everyone else in the focus group, these can add to the amount of data that would otherwise be gathered from eight or twelve individuals if they were interviewed separately.

More information can be obtained at one time since there might be anywhere from eight to twelve people in a group being interviewed. There are a greater number of intelligent thoughts and perspectives in a group than would be offered with a single interview or what the researcher may consider on his or her own.

Focus groups have minimal interviewer effects. The driving force behind this type of group discussion is interaction between the participants; the moderator exerts only a modest steering force on the overall direction of conversation. This is why a respondent will be less apt to try to figure out the objective of the study or to make attempts at pleasing the moderator.

Spontaneity is more probable in a focus group. It is essential that the participant in the interview study actively listens and gives responses to all questions. However, in a group setting, participants may feel that it is not necessary to talk if they do not wish to. This lack of pressure most frequently enables group participants to act more spontaneously and enthusiastically.

A typical result of focus groups is also quality interviewing because if a number of individuals are being interviewed concurrently, the research group can afford to hire an expert moderator. This is a crucial point since the role of the moderator is essential to the interview's success.

Focus group interviewing allows the interviewee to be in a more comfortable setting. Solo interview situations are not particularly natural. A researcher can design a much more casual atmosphere within a focus group. Participants might think of this more as a real world setting and their comments and responses will be more natural and realistic.

Guidelines for Focus Groups

By adhering to several basic guidelines, high-quality focus group interviews can be obtained.

Make sure the group stays small, usually between eight and twelve people. Jeff Bezos of Amazon would suggest his pizza rule: If you cannot feed your group with two pizzas the group is too large. When a group is too small it will not have sufficient input to be of value, and it is possible for one or two people to dominate the study. On the other hand, when you have a larger group, frustration and boredom are found more frequently as not all members are able to have adequate talk time. In a larger setting, there might be "social loafers" who will not participate at all and "hide behind" the others who are participating.

Selection should proceed with caution so that the correct participants are involved. Relatively homogeneous, focus group members should have the same values, experiences, and verbal skills and so that some members do not intimidate others. Individuals with prior group experience should be dropped, and members should not already know each other. Many larger cities have businesses that will recruit focus group members according to precise qualifications they have set for a task.

> *Make sure the group stays small, usually between eight and twelve people.*

See that the atmosphere in the group session is very natural and as benign as you can make it. A respondent's home or a hotel room are some of the optimal sites for a focus group. A lot of researchers will have a focus group space at their office complex, too, equipped with refreshments, comfortable seating and very few distractions.

The session should last no more than two hours. Once you have reached the two-hour mark, participants quickly become bored and fatigued.

Find the most qualified moderator that you can afford. A moderator guides and focuses the conversation and catches any subtle points that need to be elaborated upon. A competent moderator draws out the timid participants and can inhibit those members who are trying to dominate the conversation. Encouraging participants to engage in actual discussion rather than responding to the moderator, as well as knowing when a discussion needs to be ended, are hallmarks of an excellent moderator. In conclusion, the facilitator must assess and evaluate the discussion when it is completed.

Tape every session if possible. By taping the session, the moderator is free to concentrate on the dynamics of the group and way monitor shifts rather than committing details to memory or taking notes. When a permanent archive like this exists, it lets a researcher return to the tapes to get more insight or clarity.

It is important that others be able to hear and observe the group undetected; therefore, two-way mirrors must be made available. That is often an option only in focus group rooms that are specially built on the premises of ad or research agencies. Two-way mirrors let other focus group specialists to observe the proceedings and share in the concluding interpretation.

Establish defined objectives for every session, using a set agenda of topics whenever possible. Although the discussion of a focus group session will eventually zero in on the researcher's primary point of interest, it will normally start with a more general discussion (e.g., before talking about child-rearing hygiene, some general talk about parenting will occur).

If funding is not an issue, the researcher should hold a number of group discussions. A few of the extra focus groups should be composed the same as the original group, but others need to be very different. Good focus groups are not necessarily without some cost, however, as they can cost anywhere between $2,000 and $5,000.

Mall Intercept

Mall interviews are probably the next most popular strategy for conducting business surveys in the U.S., after phone interviews. Significantly reducing travel costs and keeping the interviewer perpetually busy with questioning, they are relatively inexpensive since interviewees come to the interview rather than vice versa. There is still a concern about sample quality when it comes to mall intercepts, despite the method's efficiency. This is where two issues may arise. Initially, it is advised that people visiting a mall do not represent the population desired by the researcher. Another larger problem with this technique is that interviewers can introduce bias by selecting an unrepresentative sample of people, favoring those who are: by themselves, without friends or family to distract them; similar to the interviewer in some demographic sense, whether in terms of social standing, sex, age, or race; obviously unoccupied; or simply, in the interviewer's opinion, especially pre-disposed to participate in the study.

Sampling frame bias is the chief concern using this approach. Almost every household has at least one annual shopping mall visit, and two-thirds of these have visited in the last two weeks. That means the problem is that when the researcher hopes for a result that can be projected, how does one deal with the fact that some people just shop at malls more frequently than others? Two tasks can be done in a mall study in order to handle this issue. The first thing is that malls within the area can be chosen on the basis of probability that its selection will be proportionate to the amount of people statistically served. Secondly, there needs to be a procedure created so that individuals can be sampled randomly within each mall that is been chosen. If performed properly, a procedure like it would assume that everybody in the mall has, over a given period of time, the same probability of being picked for the sample. Nonetheless, the more a given person visits shopping malls, the better his or her probability of getting chosen. That means the researcher has to think about how often a person goes to the mall and let that enter into the weight of the answers.

A surveyor selecting persons for a shopping-mall sample representation can unwittingly undermine the results of a meticulous study by their choice of a complacent subject. Luckily, the potential of interviewer bias can be combated by developing a procedure that is very tightly specified and does not allow the interviewer any freedom of choice in interviewees. That process necessitates choosing a few random entrances and then interviewing each seventh or tenth - or whichever number has been selected--person who arrives at the chosen entrances. A few different doors have to be used since various types of shoppers park at various entrances to the mall (if they do not arrive by public transportation or a ridesharing service) and since different types of customers are often attracted to different types of anchor stores. Lastly, the researcher needs to be fastidious about doing interviews in the mall on various days and various times of the day. It bears restating that the best practice is to correlate the days and times chosen for interviews with the mall's anticipated amount of customer traffic in that time period.

On the contrary, mall surveys can often yield satisfactory population estimates with the added advantage of face-to-face interviewing at costs the low-budget researcher can afford if the sampling procedures outlined are followed and proper weighting is utilized. Not every mall will allow people to be interviewed in the mall, and some will limit interviews to those businesses that lease a permanent site to do this on the premises. In the latter, it might still be financially feasible to have the researcher on a tight budget to be in touch with the services of these agencies.

Lastly, malls have a big advantage over personal interviews in the home: larger displays can be set up, commercials can be running, and high-tech equipment can take measurements. For instance, it is a relatively simple matter for an auto maker to display several test models at a mall where respondents have a chance to study them and form useful opinions, whereas the idea of the manufacturers providing the same resources for an in-home preview to individual interviewees is laughable.

SAMPLING FRAMEWORK

Quota Sampling

Quota sampling is a common method for containing expenses in commercial market research. That process is frequently combined with interviews obtained at the mall and, in addition, is quite common in phone studies. This strategy is quite easy to use, very affordable, and can give almost the same results as those that might be found using a probability sampling.

The process is simple when creating a quota sample; the researcher simply creates a profile of the group to be studied and then requires interviewers to reach quotas for the final sample to fit with the main characteristics of the group profile. If the quotas are complex enough and the interviewers are directed not to interview only the easy or convenient individuals, the results can be projected as any probability sample, and the costs will be dramatically lower than other procedures. A key factor to saving money is to make sure the workers know they do not have to fret about refusals from potential participants and just keep seeking interviews from whoever will cooperate until the quotas are filled.

Quotas can be utilized in phone studies to set up controls for possible biases in those that do not respond. The biggest risk involved in quota sampling is having the ending sample participants chosen by the fieldworkers. Should the fieldworkers have a bias to start with, then naturally the research that results will have a bias. Careful control and systemization of the process is the easy way to get inexpensive but good-quality quota research.

Convenience Sampling

Researchers find mall intercepts extremely useful because they allow respondents to engage in the interviewing process at their own discretion and also because they make it easy to get a representative sample for most target populations. Convenience can be an overriding concern in several instances. There are four circumstances in which convenience samples could serve a purpose. To begin with, few rare cases exist where a sample result can be generalized to produce a projected statement. Secondly, in experiments that call for control situations and treatments to be introduced to the subject set at random, researchers will find convenience sampling ideal. Third, when the researcher is simply looking to create exploratory data, convenience samples can be the ideal option. Lastly, if a researcher wants to do in-depth interviews, convenience samples can be utilized.

Studying these types of people can be extremely beneficial when investigating the convenience population is one of the researcher's concerns. Natural examples might be a project that studies those who patronize the services of the client organization, those who patronize one mall or center, or those who work at a particular place or pass by a particular spot. There are studies in which any respondent will do. In the exploratory studies, this is frequently the case. For example, it can be assumed that the relationships between sets, age, and experience, are similar from one person to another.

Convenience Experimentation

As long as the target population is not composed of obviously rare or exceptional people, convenience sampling is a great way to test new products, advertisements or packaging options, as well as to gather feedback on sensory impressions such as feel, smell, and taste. The researcher just has to create a process for assigning subjects to various treatments randomly and then make certain that stimuli are not presented without being carefully controlled. In addition, they have to make certain that participants do not talk to each other during or right after the study.

QUALITATIVE RESEARCH WITH CONVENIENCE SAMPLES

The employment of convenience samples is beneficial for a number of qualitative research projects. Some of the useful information that can be gathered is an understanding of people's preferred terms to use in describing a particular object, the features of that object they pay attention to or the reasoning that drives their decisions on a particular topic; convenience samples can also help with the development of new questions for use in upcoming questionnaires. When a questionnaire needs to be pre-tested for use in a later study, this method is also useful. This allows the researcher to isolate issues with the materials, identify cases where the situation or models used are too unrealistic to provide useful data, and to see whether the message is portrayed in the manner intended. In addition, the convenience sample may be employed to develop hypotheses to be tested later on. The one thing regarding a qualitative study is that you should not study those who have special traits, particularly those that know something about the topic.

Interviewing In-depth with Convenience Samples

Many researchers swear by the great value of interviewing small numbers of individuals in great depth because firmly-held convictions, unexpected meanings, and core fears and desires are exposed through the process that the researcher might never uncover through questionnaire surveys or group discussions. Specifically, the advantages of doing in-depth interviews instead of using focus groups:

There is no requirement by the respondent to accommodate the researcher or to be concerned with personal choices or comments.

Interviewing in depth is of particular value when sensitive subjects are being dealt with.

The one responding is then the whole focus of the interviewer and may very well open up more easily.

The interviewer is directly involved in the process, so the respondent is generally very focused, leading to richer data that is more easily applicable to the study.

The available time for a single respondent to speak, most likely in a focus group, is short. The common hour and a half or more in an in-depth interview time frame allows a participant to share information that is usually broader and deeper than information gathered from just a focus group.

Interviewing in depth is of particular value when sensitive subjects are being dealt with. For example, interviews with elderly individuals who are toward the end of their life and with groups who are concerned about anonymity.

Sought After Sampling

It may sometimes be to the researcher's advantage to look for particular respondents since their responses could turn out to be good predictors of the things the general populace would speak, think, or feel. In order to create a forecast, a researcher will question those in positions of power within various industries or sectors. Conversely, they might concentrate the interviews, too, in a part of the nation or world that represents the target market or can be seen as indicating future trends. For instance, political analysts check on key precincts to help themselves with election forecasts.

Key informants are an additional sampling that marketers frequently use. In many areas, such consultants can frequently offer the best trend data and can give detailed descriptions of current market activity. In order to gain a better understanding about possible future developments, it is common for many organizations to send a staff member to interview such well-informed individuals in considerable depth. Interviews like these produce insights that can be very helpful for marketers. The important factor here is commitment to a regular and consistent manner of interview.

Judgment samples have two big problems associated with them. First, it is possible for there to be selection bias when researchers are tempted to select participants who are quite approachable. Second, when experts are hired, there is the possibility that they will become too familiar with the topics and will not be able to hold onto their objectivity.

Network Sampling

High costs and poor efficiency are common to several of the methods used to conduct general-population probability sampling. A large, random telephone survey, for instance, would be of little help to a researcher that wanted to concentrate on issues affecting paraplegics. Call screening is the usual way researchers deal with this challenge; the viability of a potential respondent selected at random is verified with a series of questions before the proper survey begins. Some researchers, during some studies, will pay the high screening cost in order to get a set of results they can use.

Nevertheless, there are instances in which the research focuses on a subject that would make screening too costly because of the large number of respondents who would not be eligible. This can be an excellent time to use network sampling, a process that rests on the idea that individuals belong to networks with other similar individuals. This allows the researcher to contact several participants who have the required characteristics of interest and then ask them for the names of other individuals who also possess those characteristics. This is the strategy that makes use of interpersonal networks.

A convenience sample can be compared to information obtained using a similar process. For instance, should a hospital lead an attitude survey of patients that have been there, it could realize it is not learning anything about prospective new customers? This could be overcome by the hospital requesting that participants provide the name of one or two individuals who have never utilized the hospital's services. The benefits to the snowball approach has to do with the second sample being, most often, closely matched to the patient sample that already exists in terms of class and economic status.

This method works as well for studies with mainly qualitative aims.

Sequential sampling is an approach to probability sampling which yields results that can be applied to future endeavors while at the same time keeping the costs low. That will mean dipping many times into the pool of participants that has been chosen randomly and checking things after each time. However, this does not usually mean high cost, as the data most often shows consistency fairly soon so that the sampling may end. This method works as well for studies with mainly qualitative aims.

Online and mail surveys as well as in person and phone interviews are the usual actions a researcher takes, but there are other affordable strategies that can be occasionally valuable.

A self-administered survey, a combination of a mail study and in-person or telephone interview techniques is the most common. First, the respondent is asked to cooperate by the interviewer over the phone or in person (e.g., at a mall, store, office, or general public location); following consent, usually with the prospect of a financial incentive, the questionnaire is given to the respondent by hand or by mail. High service industries often utilize this strategy, which includes some natural advantages:

- Respondents may be asked in person to participate.
- Whatever questions respondents might have can be answered immediately.
- Many individuals are able to be contacted and engaged for an affordable price in terms of employee time.
- Questionnaires are not squandered away on doubtful respondents.

Health care organizations also use self-administered surveys to great effect. When patients are handed a survey to fill out, the rate of participation is high and gives hospital marketing managers very valuable tracking data. Using computer equipment is a different method of conducting a self-administered survey. Actually, a tiny percentage of people won't be familiar with computers, and the benefits to the ones who are familiar with them will be much greater.

These are some of the greatest benefits that interviews conducted via computer have to offer: It is easy to employ advanced patterns of question skipping in a manner that does not negatively influence respondents. A serious issue with mailed surveys that one self-administers is that only limited skips can be used. Skips are helpful when those responding have to be led to other parts of the survey based on their answers to particular questions. There are a lot of branching instructions needed when the questionnaire has a complex set of subcategories, but this is simplified when automated on a computer.

A respondent will not know the length of the questionnaire and so will be less likely to be overwhelmed from the very beginning.

Different from self-administered or mail questionnaires, in these the participants are not able to return to correct their answers or look ahead to find out what is coming. This aids in removing bias from the survey.

Answers without consistency are able to be corrected right then and there. These advantages apply to telephone and personal interviews as well, but it is quite difficult for interviewers to detect inconsistencies. With this connection, the computer can be considered absolutely correct in all cases.

A database can be designed that analyzes information as soon as the respondent answers. There are two payoffs for using this method. The first payoff is that a few steps are omitted in the most common research design so that errors are avoided. Secondly, the management team can obtain a summary of what is going on every day or even every hour. There are three advantages to this. First, analyzing the surveys that have been submitted can help highlight any problems the questionnaire contains. Second, there may be suggestions about additional questions. Third, having day-to-day analyses available can allow the research manager to end the study after having interviewed fewer participants than was planned originally, which reduces expenses.

On the Ground

Matt understands that even though he is working under tight economic constraints he still has to expand the knowledge base of his company in order to stay competitive. His management team requires valid research results to make their decisions and that conducting surveys and asking questions is usually crucial for understanding particular management issues.

- What do I ask?
- How do I ask them?
- Whose answers will I use and whose will I disregard?
- Will some questions need an explanation?

For instance, he is thinking the study could begin with an in-person interview and supplement that interview with an email questionnaire later for the respondent to fill out at his or her leisure with detailed information about their preference and attitudes about of non-film programming, such as sporting events. He likes the idea because of its low cost. He does not think direct mail or phone surveys are the best choice since so many people are using the Internet, and calling and mailing is much more expensive and may not be worth the additional expense.

Yes, he thinks face to face interviews are his best choice. Matt thinks customers coming into a store are generally serious and focused, and he will politely ask patrons for their opinions. He thinks patrons would be open to answering, although questions would need to be efficient. What do you think Matt should do?

Another concern is that he thinks there are different types of people that come to EA. There is the professional crowd that comes during the week. There is also the evening, full-time employed crowd that comes during the week and the weekend, and the weekend clientele.

He would like to get their opinions and is wondering the best way to get a representative sampling of each of the profiles. He is going to look over his receipts for the last three months and see how many customers he averages per day showing in each of the segments. He is wondering how many he needs to sample. How many do think he should interview? Since he wants to get a profile of an "average customer" one of the first questions he thinks he should ask is, "How many times have you come to this store in the last year or so?" What do you think may be some other good questions?

Chapter 8

LEVERAGING SOCIAL MEDIA

In this information age, it would be a mistake not to leverage this valuable resource in the process of gathering information. Unmistakably, social media has become one of the most popular vehicles for personal information and human connection. Social media market research can assist management in gathering quantitative and qualitative data across a number of social media platforms.

The probability exists that data can be efficiently collected and analyzed in order to identify market trends, consumer preferences, and socio-cultural changes.

Every account, every purchase, every view, and every click is documented somewhere. Social media is not just for celebrities like Katy Perry, Taylor Swift, and Justin Bieber. Organizations, large and small alike, have turned to social media for advertising, consumer connectivity, answering questions, taking surveys, testing products, and so much more.

Social media market research can assist the manager in gathering quantitative and qualitative data across a number of social media platforms.

A Few Statistics

There are over 3 billion active social network users in the world. In the United States alone, there are over 200 million social networks users and the number is growing daily as activity continues to see a fairly consistent increase in user interaction. Social media continues to gain strength in the area of ecommerce and marketing. In the United States, over 80 percent of the population has at least one social networking profile, and many use two, three, or more. Over 90 percent of all retail brands use at least one social media channel, if not two, three, or more. There are 60 million active business pages on Facebook alone. Instagram boasts over 800 million active users, YouTube claims that over 1 billion hours of video are watched on a daily basis, and the number of tweets sent each day is 500 million (think about that… it means about 6,000 tweets are pushed over the internet every second). Over 80 percent of small businesses use a social media platform in some way. The number of thoughts, opinions, and messages transmitted each second exceeds 41 million.

Facebook, Twitter, YouTube, Instagram, Pinterest, LinkedIn, and many other social networks allow a marketer to target an audience, interact with their consumers, and drop timely content to the world in just seconds. Social Media provides an opportunity for organizations to efficiently and effectively listen to their customers (or potential customers) like never before in history. The data collection opportunities through these networks are beyond quantifiable.

Hard and Soft Costs

Social Media Platform Costs

The cost of having and maintaining social media accounts vary with the organization's intent. There is no cost to creating an account, popping up a decent profile photo, and enter the world of social media. Posting is free, blogging is free, and commenting is free. The cost of these actions is simply time, energy, and creativity. Depending on the size of the organization, it might be advisable to hire someone to design your social media page or profile to line up with your desired "brand" or persona. This should be a onetime cost and could be as low as $200 or as high as $2,000, depending on the needs of the organization. Content development, however, may require more effort and expense. Using social media accounts for marketing, advertising, research, or ecommerce increases with every intentional practice. Identifying your marketing needs and creating a research strategy (as discussed in Chapter Three) is no different when you engage in social media activity. Driving customers to your business through social media is complex and may require a social media expert in order to be effective.

Initial Set up for Social Media Usage

While there is no cost for a typical social media profile, there are tools needed to efficiently and effectively use and maintain a social media account. Obviously, there are hardware costs such as a computer, cellphone, tablet, or whatever electronic device is necessary to maintain your platform. The assumption is that the organization already has this equipment.

There are many free tools that the business can find to assist in managing social platforms. There are social media management tools for a minimal cost, less than $100-150, that will increase efficiencies and generate performance information. The costliest, and most refined tool is what is known as the CRM system, which is perfect for a business that wishes to track all intentional social media efforts as they relate to final sales and customer management.

Creating content for social media seems at first to be a no-brainer but it certainly has its unique challenges. Content must remain interesting and useful, or it will be ineffective at its core and therefore inefficient as the user wastes time (which is a valuable resource). Good content is the key to social media success and can often require creativity, a keen sense of any unique trends, the ability communicate a message succinctly, and often, additional skills in photo software. The photos, text, wording, style, and general subject matter will depend on the organization's culture, brand, and persona as well as the level of professionalism desired. The cost of using photos can range from the use of a simple cell phone to a professional camera set up. Free apps are available for creating infographics, but a software package such as Photoshop may be required for a more professional and unique design. These content creators are determined by what the business can afford and the social media budget.

Advertising and Exposure

Here is where costs can begin to add up. Reaching the right people, getting the message out, and driving business back to your page can be as inexpensive as a do-it-yourself ad (for as little as $50) or a comprehensive advertising plan using a wider 'net' to reach more people more often (costing anywhere from $1,500 to $150,000 or more). Running ads can drive sales and activity, while an effort toward building brand awareness may require wider engagement and a more continuous effort, and therefore, higher costs. Once again, as with all other marketing undertakings, this must all be determined during the budgeting phase.

Outsourcing to a Social Media Professional

Creating a strategy is critical and outsourcing or hiring a social media manager is costly but may result in a higher return on investment of time and financial resources. Just as with all other marketing efforts, it is necessary to use measures to view a clear picture of the impact or return on the effort or cost. Using the measures provided on most social media accounts (insights, analytics, etc.) is free, but understanding the numbers and drawing conclusions may require a professional social media company or a social media manager. These professionals are trained to manage your social media platform in order to generate more leads, grow the business, increase sales, or any other targeted purpose – all by engaging and connecting customers to your business. The cost could range from simple engagement to a full-blown media strategy – ranging from $2,000 to $10,000. Once again, this effort can usually be al-a-carte or by the package and the cost can range from a flat fee for a typical set up for a small business, and/or the addition of a monthly fee for management (depending on requests, a range from $500 a month to $5,000 for a small business). A social media consultant who will track and analyze data, convert it to useful information, and make recommendations, and produce measurable results can cost $100 to $500 per hour. The social media management business is competitive, so if the manager does the hard work of 'shopping' for just the right organization, the return on investment could be extensive.

> *These professionals are trained to manage your social media platform in order to generate more leads, grow the business, increase sales, or any other targeted purpose – all by engaging and connecting customers to your business.*

It is imperative to remember when utilizing this service to clearly state your objectives and make sure the expert has a firm understanding of how your business operates.

SOCIAL MEDIA AND MARKETING RESEARCH

Traditional market research can be costly and time consuming. It takes time to set up surveys, focus groups, sampling, data collection, etc. Face it, it can also be difficult to find enough people to provide input for usable data and reliable statistics. Social media can provide the researcher with information in hours (or even minutes). Using social media as a tool for gaining insights can reduce the use of resources (increasing efficiency) and assist a business with effective market research features such as customer insight, brand appearance, market changes, and much more. Your social media network probably consists of current customers, almost customers, target customers, and influencers in the industry. An important step in using social media for research is to plan the right strategy to get the measurable information and results you need and knowing the benefits of using this method of research.

A Few Benefits of Social Media Marketing Research

- *Cost Efficient Research* – Using social media for business market research is an investment of time. In most cases, this time and effort is all the researcher needs to gather data and derive useful information. Again, when comparing this to traditional research methods (studies, experimentation, surveys, focus groups, etc.) the cost variance is astounding. Social media platforms provide free tools to assist in the gathering of information. Learning to analyze that information may take time (and often professional assistance), but overall is a most cost-efficient way to collect information.
- *Real-time Insight into Trends* – Facebook, Twitter, Pinterest, Instagram, and most other social media platforms offer different ways to take a pulse on trends and provide opportunities for research. A simple search of current terms, hashtags, latest trending subjects, and high-performance posts can give real-time notifications of anything related to your industry, business, or interests. An instant notification could be sent any time a customer or competitor uses these terms.
- *Expand the Scope of Inquiry* - The number of users on social media gives the researcher an instant 'pool' of respondents that could fit the marketing strategy focus. The statistics stated in the beginning of this chapter indicates a clearly popular vehicle for connecting people, businesses, and information. The social media audience is so much larger than one you can find in any single location, information source, or media platform.

- *Honest Responses* – Social media has a strange way of bringing out opinions, engaging users, and promoting interaction. Users are casual and quick in many of their responses. Getting a 'first reaction' response can often be the most effective way to obtain accurate data.
- *Observation Juxtaposed to Information* – Gathering data or information via a study, experiment, survey, interview, or any other traditional method of collection is typically led by focused and specific questions, which must be designed carefully (with an outcome in mind). The design of those questions may result in a totally different answer (as we learned earlier in the chapter) depending on how the question is worded. In addition, being so focused can cause the myopic determination for an answer and may cause the researcher to miss opportunities for unplanned discovery of insights or trends. Observing market trends, social issues, current events, customer preferences, etc., can give the researcher valuable insight from a vast audience.
- *Real-time Interaction* – Carefully planned studies and experimentation are excellent ways to collect data, but in the uncertain environment in which planning takes place, some important research might be missed. Social media platforms offer real-time interaction with your market. Research is timely. Information is up-to-date. Current events or changes in the general or task environment are quickly identified.

Social Media Research Options

By now you cannot deny the value of social media and its potential to be an efficient and effective marketing research tool. If you have decided to integrate or begin assimilating social media research into your approach, here is a menu of options you can consider.

- *Identify the Competition (and see what they are up to)* – Your competition is likely using at least one social networking site. Just by tapping into these social media platforms, you will be able to find noteworthy facts about your competition just by paying attention. Monitoring Facebook posts, tweets, or blog posts is a cost-effective method to know what people say about your competitors. Simply watching and thinking critically about how you can 'do better' will give insight into ways your organization compares to a competitor.
- *Monitor Customer Satisfaction* – Customer responsiveness is one of the critical building blocks of competitive advantage. Being able to engage directly with customers allows your organization to directly address problems, questions, and analyze feedback at a much faster rate than other methods of connectivity. Send direct messages (DM) to customers only when they ask questions or have a complaint or concern. If you choose to ask them a question, be sure to have a valuable incentive or you may just annoy customers. More about monitoring this in "collect feedback."
- *Track Key Words* – Social Media is a central place to track key words about your organization, your competition, your industry, similar industries and products, etc. One simple and efficient way to research key words or thoughts is the utilization of hashtags, affectionately known by the #. Even a simple Internet search using a hashtag will provide the researcher with a number of exploration and observation possibilities. One of the most relevant is information on what is currently trending. For example, type #fitness, #photography, or #dog in your search bar and see what is trending on social networks. Start searching for things related to your business and head to those social media networks to see what is current and trending.
- *Demographic Research* – Understanding the market demographics will help you define your best target audience or target respondents. Social Media platforms will allow you to customize your search, questions, or content accordingly. This is important as

you can then make more significant connections and build deeper relationships. Target the customers that matter the most to you. Most Social Media platforms include a tool that resides right on their site to allow you to see comprehensive demographic information and data related to your target audience.

- *Audience Insights* – You can view data about your target audience and make more decisions based on what is most relevant. To increase efficiency, reports can be run regularly and sent directly to your email. For example, Facebook can provide insights based on demographics:

   - Age and Gender
   - Relationship Status
   - Education Level
   - Employment Role
   - Top categories
   - Page Likes
   - Top Cities, Countries, and Languages
   - Device Users

Facebook also uses third party data and can also provide valuable information about:

   - Lifestyle
   - Household Income and Size
   - Home Ownership
   - Home Market Value
   - Spending Methods and Behavior
   - Retail Spending
   - Online Buying Behavior
   - In Market for Specific Items (furniture, vehicle, etc.)

Accessing audience insights allows you to filter your audience with the overall platform audience. Once you define your audience by using this information, you can save it for later use or modification. This saves time and energy!

- *Collect Feedback by Listening* – Collecting customer feedback is vital to the communication and connectivity process. We typically default to taking traditional surveys when we want feedback. Social Media is, again, a valuable resource for research and gathering valuable customer feedback. Through social media communities, you can deliver efficient customer support and gather effective feedback. You must listen carefully and stay well-informed of what customers are saying about you on social media - your other customers and potential customers certainly are! When people turn to social media to vent their complaints, word spreads like a wild fire. Make sure you monitor anything someone says about your organization and that of your competitors. Respond swiftly to anything negative. Not only is this customer responsiveness, but there is value in hearing the criticism and knowing what customers in general might be unhappy about.
- *Collect Feedback through Surveys and Polls* - Ask people in your social network to share their opinions on a critical issue (or a curious question about preferences) through a survey or poll. Most social media platforms have this feature. If they do not have the capability, you can post a link on your platform that will take people to a survey on the internet. For little cost, you can build a survey on a survey generator such as Survey Monkey, Polldaddy, SurveyNuts, etc. Some of these online survey builder tools limit the number of responses you can gather.

Your question or survey does not need to be about a critical issue -- it can be a lighter question that helps give you context about your customers' preferences and opinions. For example, ask a question or take a poll on Twitter to get an idea of how customers feel about packaging. Perhaps something as simple as, "Hey, quick poll! Tell us one word that describes how you feel about our new packaging (or pricing)." You can assess more quantitatively by asking, "How many times do you go out to eat in a typical week?"

Your research can be completed in one day and the result can be as simple as:

> 20%→None
> 55% → 1-5
> 25% → 5+
> Number of responses: 209
> 18 people are talking about this

This type of quick survey can provide immediate information to the department responsible and adjustments can be made if necessary.

Collect Feedback Ahead of New Roll Outs

Collect customer feedback prior to the rolling out of new products or features. It is better to get feedback and analysis before you launch because you may have time to adjust or improve something if the customer identifies an issue. This may prevent a flood of criticism and negative posts.

Focus Groups on Social Media

You can segment your social media network to perform effective focus groups. Most networks have the functionality to segment the population by location, industry, preferences, etc., in order to target your question(s). Hangouts, conferences, Q&A sessions are just some of the methods you can use to implement a focus group. Social Media platforms are changing almost daily and are responding to the need for this feature. Facebook Live is just one example that is relatively useful for suggestions generated by users. Questions and comments are made and can be collected and analyzed after the session has ended.

A good number of organizations have several social media accounts to use not only for marketing their product or service, but also for research and recon capability. Some researchers would advise that the manager should identify which social media account is most active and relax their effort on that one and strengthen the others. Many social media and marketing experts would disagree with that viewpoint. They believe that you can detect which account is more active and gets the most traffic and take advantage of the opportunities with that channel. However, you must not neglect the others. Do not let your strength become your weakness. Consider this: You are a baseball player having trouble hitting curve balls. The next week at practice you focus primarily on hitting curve balls, and by the end of practice you are crushing the curve ball and feeling confident about the next game. The following day you get pitched fast balls and you cannot hit them. You strike out. Your strength has now become your weakness. Balance your strengths and weaknesses and do not neglect the strong and healthy platform with the most traffic.

On the Ground

Matt and his team have decided to leverage social media in order to efficiently and effectively gather some real-time information at low cost. Matt, being fairly unfamiliar with how to use social media effectively, decides to go ahead and hire an intern from a nearby university who is currently in the marketing program. With assistance from professors, Matt finds a student who is particularly interested in and proficient at social media research. The student, Eva, is excited to use her training to assist Matt in his research. Eva gives Matt some quick ideas to get him started while she builds her research plan. First, Eva recommends that Matt take some time to do some relationships analysis by searching Facebook, Twitter, and Instagram for his competition and begin looking at interactions on a few social media platforms. In addition, she suggests he increase the scope to include the industry at large.

Matt starts by searching some hashtags. Eva confirmed that this search would yield observation possibilities on what is trending in the industry. He pokes around at #carparts, #carrepair, #automotivemaintenance, and #AutoPartsAssociation. He finds his competitors in the area and decides to look into their activity feeds. These feeds and content gives him a good idea of the trends, concerns, and reviews of his competition. Matt was surprised by the low number of followers, likes, friends, and responses to posts that one of his competitors has. The other competitor, however, is very active on social media and has over 1000 followers on Facebook alone. He decides not to ignore the inactive competitor completely, but for today he focuses on the larger one. Matt also decides that he needs to "step up his game" on social media and consider hiring a social media marketing expert. But, for now, he focuses on his research. He is surprised by the information he was able to obtain just by scrolling and viewing engagement. Matt was able to identify customer concerns and requests. Matt sees some complaints about the customer service at his competitor's store in both Mountainview and Hildale. He takes note of the complaints and decides to have his managing director, Mark, begin focused development on customer responsiveness. He knows he can gain the competitive advantage here! Matt also noticed a lot of questions concerning maintenance (particularly from younger adults). Knowing the demographic of the location of his store in Hildale (college students and young families) he takes special note of this.

Matt decides to take a survey and get some real-time feedback from customers and potential customers. He formulates a survey and carefully words his questions to get focused responses to find out customer preferences and habits. Eva then ads this to his social media platforms using Survey Monkey and begins to collect the data in a report for Matt. Eva brilliantly gives an incentive for filling out the survey and providing an email address.

Eva also trains Matt to pull reports (through insights) and identify the demographic information of his social media followers. This helps him decide what theme to use for his events.

Matt is well underway in just a short amount of time, and is able to gather real-time information, not only on his competitors and customers, but on some industry influencers. He can now use this information and add it to other information he has collected from non-social media research. Matt can now focus on his ideas for themed events and increasing sales.

Eva creates a long-term social media research plan for Matt including focus groups, additional surveys, and collecting feedback before rolling out events or products. Bonus for Matt, Eva also gives some suggestions for marketing on social media once Matt completes his research. Eva plans to coordinate "Facebook Live" events in real time right before Everything Automotive hosts their events.

Chapter 9

WORKING WITH RESULTS

Questioning is a natural function for most people, but there can be many overwhelming circumstances that challenge or taint a complete research project. The basic aim is simple and critical: a researcher must capture the honest truth. As time goes on, a researcher might like to think the results he or she is getting are being validated by what the study is showing. Results can be affected in several ways by major or minor bias on the part of the researcher.

Consider how hard it is to measure the preferences of a target audience. Imagine that a household in California contributes to three charities they support. In this case, the subject's number-one favorite is the American Red Cross, and they also give to the American Cancer Society and the American Heart Association, slightly preferring the latter to the former.

Any of the following could cause error in the measurement:

- A respondent tries to give an answer based upon how that person thinks the question is written.
- If the respondent does not understand the question or does not have an individual preference, he or she may answer the question incorrectly.

- The question may have been vaguely worded or might not accurately demonstrate the objectives of the study.
- Possible interviewer errors could lead to an inaccurate response and then include the accidental recording of an inappropriate symbol or number, misinterpretation of the respondent's meaning, or other simple mistakes in understanding the respondent.
- The data entry individual may input erroneous information into the computer mistakenly.

Whatever statistical trickery is used on the spoiled information, the ultimate result will be "garbage" rather than the truth.

"Garbage in, garbage out" is the inevitable effect when any of the above-mentioned events taint the researcher's data. Whatever statistical trickery is used on the spoiled information, the ultimate result will be "garbage" rather than the truth. Returning to the functional approach used from Chapter Four, before addressing the difficulties involved in securing and recording actual individual responses, we will cover errors arising from mistakes in coding or data entry.

SOURCES OF ERROR

Outside the Questions

Delivering an appropriate question to the research subject is just part of the researcher's challenging task; building up an accurate picture of the interest group's true responses and opinions is equally important. It is certainly a challenge to set the question up correctly, but that will not guarantee that the data respondents give will be put accurately into a database or that it will be properly analyzed.

Data Entry Errors

Data entry errors frequently occur in large studies and can greatly compromise it; however, these errors can be almost eliminated by verifying every entry. The following are possible remedies for data error:

- At the beginning, a layer of data entry can be cut out entirely if respondents can enter their answers directly into a computer, whether through using a terminal in a face-to-face interview or through taking an online survey (interviewer errors are also mitigated by these methods).
- Secondly, when there are two or more data entry people, a sample of the surveys that each one enters should be verified to find out if any one of them will require 100 percent verification. The computer can also be instructed to automatically find suspicious entries where values fall outside of a question's valid range or present apparent contradictions (e.g., someone who does not report taking medication but does report a serious health condition that requires it). Lastly, if the assumption is that the errors in entry are random, then they can be accepted as just random data noise.

Mistakes in Coding

Coding is the process of assigning numerals, words, or symbols to something. Any occurrence will have various types of values that can be assigned to what is observed or asked about. Numeric appraisals are the crude data for probably 99% of all retail investigative studies and all samples where data assessments or populace estimates are to be made. When using questionnaires, coding can be done at different stages of the research and can be done by various people. There exist three options with regard to coding. One possibility is that answers that have been pre-coded, such as in online, mail, or self-report surveys, can be checked by the participant. The second possibility is that an interviewer can check pre-coded answers via the telephone or an interview. Lastly, answers that are post-coded mean that codes are assigned by a third party with regard to the things that were written down by the respondent or the interviewer.

There would be a big advantage to research if there were pre-coded answers that were able to be validated right there by the respondent or by the interviewer. There are a few benefits to pre-coding, like lessening the mistakes made recording and allowing a phone interviewer to ask questions more speedily during a set time period, which results in more answers. Respondents will be more likely to participate in a pre-coded questionnaire delivered through the mail or via self-reporting because it appears simple. In addition, it allows information to be put into the computer right from the questionnaire.

Sometimes pre-coding will assist in clarifying a question for the one answering. For instance, it could show the level of detail that the researcher is seeking. When the question that he or she hears is, "Who did you consult to resolve your health issue?" a respondent has a variety of possible avenues in which to reply: He or she could describe a general source of knowledge or reference a friend, relative, or doctor by name. Giving pre-coded answers will aid in showing precisely what is intended. Additionally, it may spur somebody to answer a question which he or she otherwise might not. Simply asking respondents to state their annual household income for the previous year can be extremely off-putting, and refusals to answer this question would be common. Asking them to choose an income bracket out of a selection will get a much higher - though not universal - response. Also, when pre-coding is done it makes certain that every respondent receives the same question. Imagine that respondents are asked to answer a question about the convenience of a few different health clinics. As we said in the previous chapter, there are respondents who may think about convenience as it relates to the number of entrances in a building, parking spaces, or the amount of time it takes to travel from home.

In order to ensure that all respondents are evaluating the word "easy" in the same way, you can present them with a list of choices describing a location's travel time - "less than 5 minutes away," "6-10 minutes away," and so forth. Employing these types of pre-coded questions has two primary risks.

The first is that this strategy presumes a researcher knows the possible answers right from the start. Although it is always possible to have an "other" category on a survey, most people who respond will not fill in anything that is not listed. Second, pre-coding can lead to frustration on the part of a participant who feels that the categories do not fit their opinion or do not allow them the necessary degree of freedom to respond. For example, someone could be asked whether he or she considers that the CEO is doing a good job for the company, and if there is only a yes or no answer, some respondents might like to answer a "Yes, but..." or "Well, not as such, but..." This frustration can cause the one being interviewed to stop an interview or fail to send back a mail or Internet survey.

After the questionnaire comes back with answers, the researcher does what is called "post-coding." Here are the three main conditions in which this is usually necessary:

1. The researcher is unaware of the categories that will be used. For example, when the researcher is harried or is on a tight budget, it might not be possible to lead any initial focus groups or pre-tests so that the right pre-codes can be developed.
2. The researcher could be concerned that giving pre-coded options would bias the responses.
3. The researcher might want to collect a lot of verbatim responses that can annotate and deepen the final report.

Should a third party enter to do the post-coding, the possibility exists that a mistake will be made in assigning a code to a specific answer. The biggest problems will occur when the answers are not clear. The interviewers who complete coding right away can ask the questions that make things clear, while post-coders, who are third parties, might have to guess and estimate – but this can introduce a bias. In the majority of studies, issues with coding can be kept to a minimum by adhering to several well-accepted procedures. For instance, after a group of surveys has been completed, it is wise to review a sampling of verbatim responses and create a clear thorough set of coding categories with a few or all the potential coders. These could be recorded in a book of codes, including several instances to illustrate individual categories. It is necessary to ensure that coders know the categories and ways to use the codebook correctly.

Questions

A majority of things that threaten measurement validity that we have covered so far are somewhat or totally controllable. However, even when there is little control, this bias potential is small in comparison to the problems that pop up when trying to get truthful answers from respondents. There might be problems with the interviewer, with the respondent, or with the instrument.

Interviewers that are dressed oddly or wear too much makeup can obtain information on the phone but will probably not be effective in a face-to-face setting.

Interviewer-Induced Error

The interviewer's attitude, tone, or phrasing can lead respondents to provide a report that is false or exaggerated. The questioner could lead the survey taker to exhibit hyperbole, deceit, bragging, or distraction. A good rule of thumb for the person posing the questions is to adopt an unobtrusive manner. That means interviews conducted in person need an interviewer with similar socioeconomic traits to those responding. It is important to remember that despite their motivated, enthusiastic attitude, interviewers should present a nondescript, unremarkable appearance.

Interviewers that are dressed oddly or wear too much makeup can obtain information on the phone but will probably not be effective in a face-to-face setting.

Interviewers must be mindful to not be physically and emotionally threatening to respondents and avoid verbal or non-verbal cues that may influence participant responses. Over the course of the interview, the interviewer's characteristics, style, and specific actions can influence the results when difficult questions are asked. The way a researcher gives explanations, asks for details, or encourages more complete answers may have grave consequences for the amount and quality of the information that is obtained. This is why a researcher should take a great deal of care choosing and training the phone and in person interviewers. It may be tempting on a tight budget to employ less experienced researchers to keep costs down, but the information above should most certainly have dissuaded you from that tendency.

A study will have to include comprehensive instructions for interviewers, questions coded in advance, and a scrupulous training program if amateur interviews must be used. Even so, the threats of error caused by the interviewer are considerable. An additional issue with non-professionals is the chance they will make up interviews or answers, such as those they are afraid to ask regarding income, drinking, or sexual habits.

Respondent bias takes one of four forms: Forgetting, withholding information deliberately, unintentional distortion, or simple mistakes and deliberate distortion. Forgetting is the biggest source of bias in respondents. If leading a study on retail preferences, participants might forget details like brand names or costs, meaning the results will not be as accurate. There are two techniques that can minimize this problem's effects: First, a restrictive time limit on how far back a respondent is asked to remember can constrain him or her to the period when their memory is reliable; and second, aided recall can help - but that process has the potential to add additional biases to the research. It is important to remember that, as tempting as it might be to do this as a cost-saving measure, asking for information recall further back than can be trusted can skew study data.

Framing and distributing questions appropriately can help mitigate the bias introduced by respondent mistakes. The first thing the researcher must do is be certain that every piece of data that is desired is defined clearly, maybe by using answers that have been pre-coded. Household income is one of the statistics that is often a problem. A respondent might not understand what household income includes or could forget crucial aspects of it. Even worse, various respondents could be assuming a variety of definitions that might make them seem different even when they are not. A simple questionnaire format might not be able to address every contingency, but there can be wording that specifies many of the particulars that are desired. The interviewers who conduct studies over the phone or in person can be taught about a question's true purpose during training and given instruction on how to steer their respondents toward giving complete and accurate replies.

An additional general type of respondent issues that were not intended is failing to have a good definition of how time is perceived or distorted. A study will frequently ask for a recap of past occurrences, meaning that a researcher might want to find out the amount of colds or vacations or other circumstances that a participant has experienced. The topic of a questionnaire may be "Visits to the Doctor in the last Year." However, respondents may give information for eight months instead of a year. The issue that often arises is when responders telescope their experiences within or beyond the time frame requested. It would not be an issue if everyone involved used the same time frame for telescoping, like putting eight months into six months. However, any difference will cause the study to yield inaccurate results due to artificial differences between participant answers.

In terms of unconscious biases, people do not just telescope with regard to dates. There can be distortion by respondents in additional ways. Individual participants will vary in the use of a scale of answers with some using the entire scale and others using only the middle portion of the scale. Even though many participant answers will fall in the middle, preferences can land anywhere on the continuum. "Nay-Sayers," as they are referred to, will be inclined to concentrate on the negative side of the scale and "yea-sayers," the positive side. Such systemic biases may be controlled when the computer is used to normalize a person's responses after the information has been gathered. Design is once more the only answer to this problem. It is important to craft the questions carefully at the outset, ensuring that the study has as few questions of this type as possible. Secondly, questions that require remembrance should only inquire about well-known events (for example, do not worry about finding out the number of bottles or cans of beer a participant has consumed in the past half year). And thirdly, whenever it can be done, each question should plainly restrict the beginning time of the period. The boundary varies according to the topic, the respondent, or the study date. For instance, it is wise to anchor the time period to some exact time like a holiday, the start of the school year, or the respondent's last birthday.

More difficult to determine and control would be respondents' deliberate efforts to make themselves look different than they are or like they think the researcher wants them to be. It is more difficult generally to adjust for conscious response bias since the researcher cannot be sure what the truth would otherwise have been. In order to correct for this, the participant must be aware that candor and objectivity are essential; also, the questions and interviewer can be skewed so as to decrease the risk of such distortion. It may often be helpful to state the researcher's initial guarantee of anonymity once again when especially troublesome questions are asked.

We do not intend to help readers become expert question writers. Writing survey questions that are motivational and yet truth seeking is a skill one acquires only after a lot of practice. One method for a researcher on a tight budget to efficiently get to the task of question writing is to find questions that have been used by a few other researchers that might be appropriate for the purposes of the study. Besides ensuring that the questions being used have already undergone testing, re-using previous studies' questions also allows the researcher to enhance validity by referring to the comparative response database already generated in earlier studies. The U.S. Census is a great resource for secondary data for two main reasons: the categories included in the Census are the most commonly used by researchers and secondly, because there is a large volume of information that can be used to validate primary data.

> *After composing the survey questions, it is important to conduct a peer review to ascertain that there are no inaccuracies.*

Researchers without much experience should consult with a more seasoned question writer after exhausting the possibilities of re-using questions made by others. After composing the survey questions, it is important to conduct a peer review to ascertain that there are no inaccuracies. Lastly, the survey should be tested out with different respondents.

Questionnaires are vulnerable to several potential sources of bias or other problems, such as the following:

Order Effect

Respondent's responses to questions asked towards the end of the questionnaire will be influenced by the questions they have already answered. Asking someone to rank a set of criteria, for example, to choose among alternative service outlets makes it very likely that a later request for a ranking of these same outlets will be influenced by the very criteria already listed. Unless a prior list is there, a respondent might have done the evaluation utilizing less or possibly totally different criteria. The answer in this case is to try out various orderings on the pretest to determine if the ordering makes a difference. If a difference is found then the important questions should be placed first or the researcher should rotate the questions to balance the effects. Rotating the questions involves changing the order of the questions in every other survey.

When the questionnaire order is more overt, it is known as giving away the show. The problem rarely persists after a pretest or if the instrument is given an exterior review.

Another option while developing your questionnaire is to move intrusive questions to a position that is later in the study so that there is no resistance on the part of the person being interviewed. If the researcher chooses to ask these intrusive questions, it is better to leave them for as close to the end of the survey as possible. This will ensure that the respondent feels as comfortable as possible during the majority of the interview.

Lastly, in a long questionnaire, the answers can be influenced by the order effect. As the respondents get tired, they will be giving briefer answers that are less carefully considered. The most important questions, once more, need to come early or be rotated among your various questionnaires.

Bias from Order

Presenting respondents with an array of predetermined responses from which to choose does present one significant source of potential bias - choices that appear closer to the top of the list will likely garner better ratings from the respondents. In cases like this, it is preferable to have pre-testing as well as rotation of answers in person or on the phone. A supervisor could watch the study and emphasize various pre-coded categories of answers where the interviewer should start reading alternatives - this is referred to as rotation. While this can be handled automatically with a computer-assisted survey or an Internet survey, the researcher is responsible for manually producing, printing, and distributing alternative versions of the questionnaire in the case of a mail survey.

Questions that are worded or formatted in such a way as to try to scale attitudes and preferences could be a major source of bias. When the researcher has to build a scale, the best thing to do is utilize one of the many generalized pre-tested strategies, listed hereafter, that can be tailored to that particular study.

THURSTONE SCALES APPROACH

With this approach, the researcher uses several statements regarding an interesting element such as a brand, charity, characteristic or company. The researcher then sorts them through the responses often separating them by pre-selected criteria such as personal preference. Groupings or positions are determined by the researchers so that they are at an identical distance. The objective is to create distinct categorical groupings. Then, a few opinions are picked from each group to represent each scale position. The last questionnaire gives the respondents the summary of statements, asking them to choose the one that best demonstrates what their feelings are regarding each object. This scale ultimately shows commonality in respondent groupings.

LIKERT SCALES

One issue with Thurstone scales is that they do not show how intense a respondent's position is. In contrast, when employing the Likert scale, respondents are allowed to rate their agreement or disagreement with a given list of positions (typically according to a five-point scale ranging from "5 - strongly disagree" to "1 - strongly agree").

SEMANTIC DIFFERENTIALS

An issue with the Likert Scale is that it is hard to tell where the midpoint is - and it can be a choice of those who do not know what the answer is or by those who really do not care. That is exactly why there are researchers who let respondents have a sixth choice of "do not know" which will allow that midpoint to really show their indifference. Participants are requested to rate something like a business, a nonprofit, or a brand on various factors divided into sections numbered one to nine or one to eleven. The method used to undertake this issue is to ask respondents to show where on each of the scales they think the object in question is. Semantic differentials come with a couple of common problems. One issue is confusion about whether the scale's midpoint signifies indifference or ignorance. Another issue is that anchors might not present truly opposing viewpoints – for example, which is the appropriate opposite for rich? "poor?"

STAPEL SCALES

Researchers frequently need to rate a value which does not have a clear or definite opposite; this is the problem Stapel scales are intended to resolve. An interviewer may question respondents as to the degree a specific adjective as it is applicable to something being asked. In general, it is easier to explain Stapel scales on the phone, and they do not require a lot of pre-testing, as opposed to semantic differentials.

GRAPHIC SCALES

This type of scale is most useful for those participants who test on the low end of the literacy scale. If a respondent, for instance, is shown a graphic scale in a study, whether mailed, online, self-reported, or in person, the scale in which the positions appear to be the same can be utilized. A ladder may be used by a researcher to stand for social classes, and people are requested to place themselves on it.

There are times when a study will touch on an issue that seems intrusive or threatening to a respondent. Such touchy topics are difficult to put into questions, and a respondent will often not want to tell someone else about a private matter or one that they feel uncomfortable with. Certain respondents may feel threatened or embarrassed by questions that would seem to be harmless. There are a few strategies for lowering the levels of possible threat. One is to make certain that at the beginning of the study those who respond are as objective and honest as they can be because they know the answers they give will be held in strictest the confidence. That statement should then be said again when a particular threatening question is going to be introduced. Another way to introduce an intrusive question is to simply admit and state that some questions may feel awkward or intrusive. Call it what it is. This often serves to break down the rigid replies and make the respondent more relaxed. The next thing to do when trying to ease the anxieties of the respondent is to introduce the question with a reassurance that tells them that certain questions tend to generate unique answers.

Lastly, a researcher might utilize the strategy of in-depth interviewing. At this point the interviewer makes an attempt not to ask questions that seem to intrude. The interviewer merely introduces the appropriate topic (say, for instance, usage of alcohol) and then uses unobtrusive comments such as, "Tell me more about that" and "That's interesting" to encourage the respondent to keep talking. The drawback to this approach for researchers on a budget is that it calls for considerable interview expertise, takes a great deal of time and cannot be used for large, representative samples.

Constricting questions can sometimes be a problem. If the question is restrictive, respondents may hold back information or give insufficient details. In addition, they might get so frustrated that they will end the interview. A choice of "other" should usually be included, especially when a likelihood exists that some possibilities may not have been pre-coded. Where relevant, there should be multiple choice possibilities so that individuals can report a combination of answers if that is what they mean to say.

There can be a generalization bias when participants are requested to generalize about something, particularly when it is about their own actions. It is nearly always best to ask about particular past behaviors when inquiring about behavior, rather than to let the respondent generalize. Instead of asking respondents to name their preferred radio station, the interview can ask them, "Please try to remember the last time you were listening to the radio, whether it was at home, at work, or on the road. Which station were you tuned into?" The respondent will perceive the task to be about providing facts rather than making a generalization. In these instances, an interviewer is more apt to gain objective reporting that is free of errors instead of getting generalizations.

Chapter 10

STATISTICS PRIMER

As was previously stated, management frequently looks for three kinds of data: what describes, what explains, and what predicts. They will look for answers to what something is, what caused it, or what it will become in the future. Responding adequately to such types of questions requires two steps. First, a manager has to have the appropriate valid measurements as raw material. Second, in order to make the measurements useful to managers, their true meaning has to be unearthed through accurate predictions, correct measurement of cause-and-effect, and apt summaries of the data gathered. The aim of this chapter is explaining how various types of statistics may be correctly used.

The fact that people are afraid of statistics is not rational thought, but it is certainly understandable.

Fear of Statistics - A good number of individuals shun statistics - whether from fear, insufficient knowledge, or even a knowing bias. The idea is that those who do not use statistics are unpretentious and honest, but those who use them may be trying to make simple things more complicated or are seeking to hide something. The fact that people are afraid of statistics is not rational thought, but it is certainly understandable. Sadly, the most basic truths are frequently covered over with statistics. However, it is necessary to remember that statistics can be quite an effective tool for researchers on a low budget. They can improve the ability of a manager to make decisions based on good interpretation of the available data.

DESCRIPTIVE STATISTICS

These figures and facts perform the important role of taking a large chunk of information and reducing it to more manageable bites for management to evaluate. Statistics that are descriptive, such as means/modes/ranges can be managed more easily and can therefore be of greater use. Simple frequency counts, measures of central tendency such as the mean, median, and mode, and measures of variability such as the range are included in these statistics. A majority of people are not frightened by such statistics. Standard deviation and standard error do frighten most people, however. Summary data, when compared, can lead to the illumination of information and indicate areas that need work or even actions that need to be taken, that can be difficult to glean from the study information as a whole.

A more daunting type of statistics is best known as statistical testing. Concentrating on the ways statistical tests are applied can easily intimidate the researcher; statistical theories, calculations, and hypothesis are much drier subject matter than the uses to which statistical tests are put. All of these can be summarized in one basic idea: management can be kept honest when statistical tests are used. It is always tempting to ignore the real facts in order for a researcher to find an outcome that is desired, but this can result in a manager making bad decisions because the results are biased. Therefore, managers should not be afraid of statistics but should instead be grateful that they are available for reference. Analysts would do well to use one of the many computer software packages available to generate statistics and perform the statistical testing that is needed. A computer can help researchers calculate complicated statistics, although it might also inflict damage on a study.

To utilize statistics correctly, a researcher needs to think about the kind of information the descriptive statistics will be used for.

Statistical analysis: even when analysis is quite simple (i.e., counting) every characteristic must be studied and given a value that is unique. There are times, particularly in qualitative research that uses small samples, where the value may be a word or symbol. For instance, the interviewer could allow the word yes or the plus symbol (+) to show a positive response to a product, a flavor, or firm.

Values must be assigned to each data point from the sample population before the computer can generate any summary statistics or perform any statistical analysis procedures. The sophistication of each of these different values can be wildly different; the limits of how these numbers can be manipulated are set by this sophistication level. Numbers are typically formed into groups according to four categories. They are (1) nominal numbers, (2) ordinal numbers, (3) interval-scaled numbers, and (4) ratio-scaled numbers in increasing order of sophistication.

Nominal Data

The actual number value given to a particular idea, behavior or object in many cases often has no intrinsic meaning, but there are certain common number-assigning rules that have become traditional. Nominal numbers' (which are measurements that are assigned arbitrary numbers) sole purpose in the analysis is to differentiate an item possessing one characteristic from an item possessing a different characteristic. Think, for instance, about how numbers are assigned to football players. Every player owns a number which identifies a particular player from the rest. The players' numerals permit the team manager and sports-viewers to differentiate between players and gives game officials a means for assigning a penalty to an individual player. Besides differentiation, the numbers at this point mean nothing. A braggart player might tell the media differently, but players whose numbers are in the 80s are not always better than those with lower numbers, nor do they merit larger salaries. They are apt to be quicker than the ones in the 70s, but maybe not quicker than the ones numbered 16-20 or 30-50.

Ordinal Data

Measurements can be organized through the assignment of ordinal numbers. Repliers may be asked by a questionnaire to grade charities A, B, and C. Number one would usually be the charity preferred most often, with number two and three falling into place after it. Still, the issue remains that a researcher cannot definitively know the degree to which A is the preference over B, or B over C.

Non-Parametric	Nominal (Categorical) • sex, type of car, county you live in • numbers have no numeric value; they are used as labels Ordinal (Rank) • order in a line, ranking of your favorite car, results of a horse race • numbers have numeric value, but show no certainty between values Analysis Techniques: Mode, Chi Square, Cross Tabulation, t-Test
Parametric	Interval (Thermometer) • Fahrenheit temperature, dates, level of happiness • similar to ordinal data except internals are consistent and have certainty with no true zero value Ratio (Arithmetic) • height, weight, age, length • pure numeric values - can be used in any mathematical context and have a true zero value Analysis Techniques: Mean, ANOVA, Regression, Discriminant

Figure 10.1. Numerical Categories for Statistical Analysis.

> *In many marketing analyses, the difference between data that is interval or ratio-scaled is not very important to management.*

The following two classes of information are much more sophisticated than the first two mentioned. "Non-parametric numbers" is the term for ordinal and nominal measurements that statisticians and researchers use. Interval and ratio measurements are referred to as metric (or parametric) numbers. Metric measurements are absolutely required by some of the prominent summary statistics and statistical tests. This is why it is a helpful thing, though not essential, for a researcher to use interval or ratio data if it is a possibility. History shows that presuming the data are metric, when they could actually be ranked, is not really going to contribute to major result distortions. Nevertheless, making the sounder assumption that one has generated an interval scale will usually have no material effect on any conclusions.

Interval Data

With interval data, as with ordinal data, the results are ranked according to the numbers assigned to them. In this situation, however, there is more significance to the differences between the numbers. With an interval scale our assumption is that there is a meaning to the distance or interval that separates the numbers. Remember the distinction that while ratio-scaled data always has a zero point that is known, interval data does not. A typical interval scale can be found in the Fahrenheit scale of temperature: A difference of four degrees is a difference of four degrees, no matter where it occurs on the scale. The changes were equal, but since the zero point on a Fahrenheit scale is arbitrary, we can say that if the temperature rose from 50 degrees to 60 degrees in the morning, it later dropped from 40 degrees to 30 degrees just after midnight. However, it would be silly to claim that the morning hours are two times as warm as the evening hours. Is 70 degrees twice as warm as 35 degrees? Would ten degrees be five times warmer than two degrees? Conversely, age is one characteristic that is a scale having an actual known zero. In this situation, it is possible to say with certainty that a person of forty is two times as old as a person who is twenty. In many marketing analyses, the difference between data that is interval or ratio-scaled is not very important to management.

Ratio Data

Ratio analysis is simply the calculation of pure arithmetic numbers in the statistical analysis. Numbers such as 3.2 or .08 can be mathematically analyzed using specific techniques (to be discussed later). It is important to note that not all statistical tests can be used with all of data classes. For example, you cannot use linear regression with parametric data (nominal or ordinal).

Generating too much data is an issue that can occur in a lot of research. There will be data we use just as it stands, and some that we want to connect to other pieces of information to demonstrate relationships between them. Describing the population being studied can meet requirements in resolving many different decision issues. At a minimum, just carefully reviewing the information is a good beginning for doing more complex analyses.

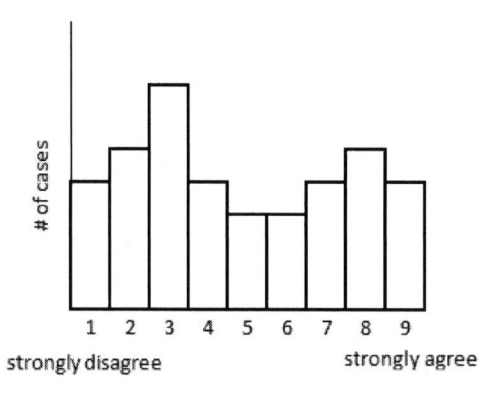

Figure 10.2. Central Tendency Observation.

There are many types of data descriptions. For instance, think about the easy scenario of evaluating a home exercise video that has just been released. In Figure 10.2, the scores that respondents give to the video as frequency distribution is portrayed graphically in bar chart or histogram. The next step is to summarize those data in a more concise structure. This becomes especially useful if the researcher needs to compare large chunks of information with each other, for example, participant ratings for three different exercise videos of ten different points each. When summarizing, there are three main features:

1. How often each selection occurs - such as how many "3" selections there were on the value-to-cost ratio for each video.
2. The central tendency measurement; For example, what was the average selection for the value-to-cost ratio selection for each video.
3. The measurement spread, i.e., did video "A" have a wider or narrower value-to-cost rating than video "B?"

Central Tendency

"Average" is a term that is used loosely by the population in general and refers to:

1. The *modal value* is the value most often mentioned.
2. The *median* is defined as the middle point in a case distribution after they have been ordered according to their values.
3. *Arithmetic Mean* is the value one gets by multiplying a value (called weighting) by the number of times it appears and dividing the resultant number by the total number of cases presented.

It is not always simple to implement a measure of central tendency. There are some other points to consider when it comes to central tendency measurements:

154   David J. Smith and Barbara A. VanderWerf

- Every possible central tendency measurement must be computed and examined. A median or mode may show you things the mean will not.
- When calculating a mode, remember that a distribution may be bimodal.
- It is a good idea for the researcher to check all responses' frequency counts or to examine a histogram (bar chart) produced by the computer in order to pick up on multiple modes when they pop up - most software packages are only going to report a single mode.
- Go ahead and make a mean computation even if the data is grouped (i.e., for young people under age ten, ten to nineteen, etc.). It is very possible for the computer software to take care of this automatically.
- When you have metric data, make certain to do a comparison of the median to the mean. Because they are the same within a normal distribution, comparing them will let you know whether the distribution you have is in any way skewed. There are statistical tests which assume that the underlying data comes close to the accepted normal curve. The more the mean and median are dissimilar, the more the distribution slants one way or another.

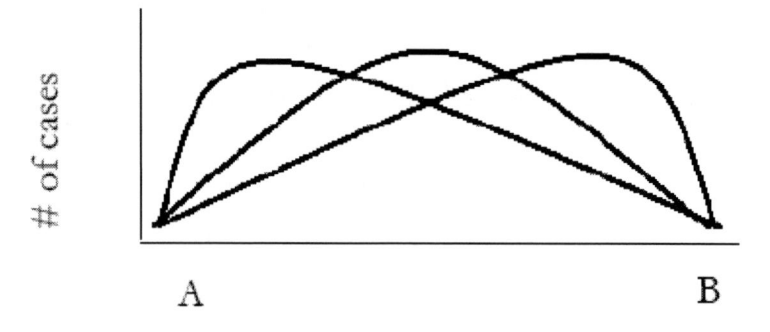

Figure 10.3. Distribution Curve Examples.

Figure 10.3 demonstrates that distributions can either be skewed positively, as in curve A, or negatively, as in curve B. Researchers can positively skew various features that marketers would be interested in, like the amount of a product that someone buys each week or what the household earns.

The relative spread of whatever information is being studied is known as measures of dispersion, a relatively underused statistic – especially by inexperienced marketing researchers. A number of important procedures in statistical analysis, such as estimating the part random chance played in experimental results, are carried out with the help of these measures.

With nominal data, there is no such thing as a measure of dispersion. Dispersion, though, can be calculated for ordinal data. Dispersion is most commonly measured over a full minimum-to-maximum spectrum, or over the difference separating the 25% and 75% cases (called the inter-quartile range). Researchers like using the inter-quartile range because it is less exaggerated than the full range - this is because both extremely high ranks and extremely low ranks are eliminated from the measurement.

The standard deviation, i.e., the amount by which its square root varies, is the standard figure used to measure dispersion in metric data, whether it is ratio-scaled or interval. To compute variance, you subtract each value from the mean of all the values, square the results, and then average these squared values (actually, dividing by one less than the number of cases). There are a couple of benefits to this variance. The first thing is that it often gives greater weight to values that are a distance from the mean than to those that are close to the mean. Thus, when differences or relationships are being evaluated statistically, this measure is a fairly strict one. It also has the virtue of allowing us to accurately predict the number of cases inside a given number of standard deviation units from the mean - assuming, of course, that distribution is normal.

In addition, it is easy to directly compare two distributions with similar units using the variance or standard deviation. For instance, there can be a comparison of how the YMCA is perceived in one city and in another using both mean and variance. The locations may have the same means but vastly different variances. This might indicate that the community center's profile is pretty clear in one particular city and rather nebulous in another. In the same way, we might compare variances within a city to see whether the club's image is more nebulous for some market segments than for others.

An additional function of the standard deviation provides information about how typical a particular situation is. A data point's typicality or a-typicality can be measured quantitatively by determining the number of standard deviations that lie between it and the mean. We might say, for instance, that Reno has per capita the highest rate of tuxedo sales in America, as a mere two percent of cities that report in sell more of them. Data normalization is the last use that veteran researchers have for the standard deviation.

This measure tracks the growth rate of a summary factor, such as a proportion or mean; in most respects it is similar to standard deviation and employed in a similar way. It has the same use and meaning as standard deviation but describes the spread of some summary measure like mean or proportions. It is possible to say something about the likelihood that the true mean is within a certain distance (in standard error units) from the mean that was actually found because the percentage of cases that fall within specific distances from the midpoint of a normal curve are expressed in standard errors.

Because it is possible that a specific case may be described as being a set number of standard deviations separate from the mean brings about another important point regarding this version measure and how it can serve researchers. People tend to differ in the proportion of a given rating scale, which is a frequent problem when comparing responses to certain kinds of psychological questions across respondents. While respondents who are extroverted might make full use of an interval scale that goes from 1 to 9, giving very high and very low scores, more introverted subjects might restrict themselves to the middle of the scale, reporting scores of 4 to 6. The computer would treat a score of 6 as being essentially the same for both if we were to compare only their raw scores.

> *Normalization is a way to ensure that many different types of variables are comparable, meaning to put them all into units of standard deviation.*

Looking at scores expressed through standard deviation tracking, instead of the raw scores assigned by respondents, is the usual way to take these common variations from person to person (or question to question) into account. This means a computer would be told to use a given scale to divide the original score of each respondent by that individual's personal standard deviation on any scale that is similar. This is known as normalizing the data.

In addition, normalization is a way to ensure that many different types of variables are comparable, meaning to put them all into units of standard deviation. This strategy is frequently taken if multiple regression equations are being employed.

The following sections provide an introduction to the most important statistical analysis strategies that a new researcher might put into practice. The strategies used should be organized based on the types of data they are appropriate for, whether nominal, ordinal, or metric. Keep in mind that the reliable researcher has to first know the concept of significance and how probable it is that this hypothesis will be rejected. Traditionally, that probability was set at either .05 or .01 according to how strict the researcher wished to be prior to accepting a positive result. However, such levels are not set in stone. Why wouldn't you use, say, levels like .035 or .045? It really is not about the information being strong enough to let us state it as the truth but instead about whether the results are sufficiently convincing so that the manager feels good about acting.

The traditional way that statisticians have handled these matters is by laying out a null hypothesis (one which is free of association and difference) well in advance of the receipt of results and by settling on an acceptable limit for the deviation of the level of statistical significance within which the hypothesis still holds true. Is this decision point always predicted by or tied to other substantive results, or is it sometimes simply assigned without justification?

A statistician is seeking to measure whether or not a specific result could possibly be attributed to chance. If there is a low probability, we could conclude that the results we received greatly vary from the anticipated results and do something about it. Imagine, though, that there has been a .20 possibility yielded by the analysis that says such results aren't actually different. The question is whether or not the manager should act in this situation or only act in the event that the difference is 5/100ths or less. What would be the proper level of significance? Classically, those who work with statistics often use the .05 or .10 significance level as the place to cut things off and decide there is a significant result.

Those analyses are usually done on one of three types of data: frequencies, means or proportions. Is a clever or colorful advertisement likely to draw more people in to buy? Do the numbers of men and women who notice billboards vary proportionately? Are mean purchase levels something that can be forecast from profession, earning and family size? There are three vital points to consider here.

First, that the utility of the results must be judged according to how they meet the manager's expectations, not the researchers'; second, that real yardstick of significance is what actions, if any, the result causes; and third, the manager's pre-conceived expectations, information and anticipated course of action have a bearing on significance just as much as statistical analysis does. For this particular case, the researcher's job is clearly to give the manager the probability of a result's significance and leave the final decision about whether or not it should influence the action to be taken up to the manager.

A probability of .15 or better is significant in some cases (for example, where risk is low and management is already leaning toward a particular course of action). In situations where there is more to lose and management isn't clear about which is best, the matter will most likely be decided at only a .04 or more. The parts traditionally played by the levels of significance around .05 and .01 are more or less meaningless to the way modern-day managers make decisions.

Non-Parametric Data Analysis

The Chi Square Test

Because variances and means do not occur with nominal data, researchers will want to look at frequency counts. Two types of questions are usually inquired about those frequency counts. The common question to be asked when a single variable is being considered is how closely the study's results correlate to the model - the distribution that was expected ahead of time. To give a hypothetical scenario, our interest might be in whether or not a target population's distribution of employment areas varies from the distribution found in earlier studies or in the population of the local urban area in general. The next kind of research wants to know if the relationship with one sample is connected to a different sample, for example, whether job choices are dependent upon what part of the country the person lives in. The right kind of statistical test to utilize for both of these kinds of analysis is known as the chi square ($x2$) test. Chi Square analysis is one of the most popular statistical tools for market research, mainly because it is particularly suited to handle both nominal data and higher-order numbers.

The Chi Square Test is very easy to comprehend and just about as simple to compute. This figuring can conveniently be done by hand or with any simple computer. The only things required are the raw frequency count (F) for every value of the variable that is being analyzed and the corresponding expected frequency (E). The Chi Square method then computes the difference between those two, squares the result and divides that by the foreknown frequency. It sums those computations on all the values (cells) for the variable to obtain the final Chi Square value. Researchers can use expected-frequency division to even out the differences between cells with many and few respondents in them and ensure that their data is weighted accurately.

> *Chi Square analysis is one of the most popular statistical tools for market research, mainly because it is particularly suited to handle both nominal data and higher-order numbers.*

When making such calculations, it is crucial to enter the correct degrees of freedom in order to determine probability. This is handled by the computer itself. With marginal totals set, the number of table cells that are unconstrained in terms of acceptable value is measured by degrees of freedom. We can determine the number of cases we would expect to see for three cells in this illustration.

Cross-Tabulations

Cross-tabulation is one of the most useful analytical tools and is a main-stay of the market research industry. One estimate is that single variable frequency analysis and cross-tabulation analysis account for more than 90% of all research analyses. Cross-tabulation analysis, also known as contingency table analysis, is most often used to analyze categorical (nominal measurement scale) data.

A cross-tabulation is a two (or more) dimensional table that records the number (frequency) of respondents that have the specific characteristics described in the cells of the table. Cross-tabulation tables provide a wealth of information about the relationship between the variables. Cross-tabulation analysis has its own unique language, using terms such as "banners," "stubs," "chi-square statistic," and "expected values."

Potential Confounds

Given that Chi Square computations react wildly to expected cell frequencies that are exceptionally small and absolute sample sizes that are very large, the researcher has to be on the lookout for two potential problems. It is generally a good idea to abandon the idea of producing a chi square for a cell with an anticipated frequency below five, so that small cell size does not introduce bias to the study. Combining cells together will adjust for this requirement. Regarding the whole sample size, it winds up that Chi Square is exactly proportionate to the amount of cases that are used to calculate it.

In these circumstances, experienced researchers using large samples often depend upon statistical coefficients. It can be easy to overlook the possibility of exaggerated Chi Squares with large samples so a researcher must be cautious when comparing chi squares where the difference in significance levels is simply due to the difference in sample sizes.

The t-test is the statistical testing tool that is most often utilized after that. With a pair of population estimates, like proportions or means, the odds of both of these representing the same overall population can be found with this parametric test - although it can only be used with ratio or interval data. The computation varies based on if independent or non-independent measures are being analyzed.

t-Test

Comparing means and/or proportions from two different samples is what the t-test is used for. For instance, a t-test can show if a donor sampling in New York donated more than a similar sampling in San Antonio. In order to employ this test properly, the first step is to estimate the total standard errors that these means will have, using a rigidly-defined method. The researcher can find the combined standard error applicable to the difference in means by using the combined standard error to divide the means' difference. That shows the number of standard errors on which the two means differ. The resulting number is referred to as a "t statistic" for a small (less than 30) sample size, or a "z statistic" for a large one. That statistic lets something be known about how probable it is that two means are exactly equal (taken from a generalized group of all customers). When they are quite different, a low probability will be in evidence. Two proportions could be compared rather than two means in order to do the same analysis.

Independent t-tests are also helpful in taking care of two additional things frequently needed in the research process. They are vitally useful for gauging whether an individual sample's proportion or mean deviates from the value researchers expect. For instance, a researcher could conclude whether the average household size in a sample matches that in the Bureau of the Census for the neighborhood. Confirming that a multiple regression equation's coefficients actually equal zero is something that the test can confirm using similar reasoning.

Comparing means and proportions from one question's answers to those resulting from another of the study's questions - or from another study on the same sample group - is something that researchers occasionally need to do. These two measures are not independent, as this process would be comparing those who respond to themselves. In this instance, a computer computes the difference between every pair of answers offered by the respondent.

The different regression equations that are used to provide a set of significant predictors of a given phenomenon will be indicated by the t-statistics (together with their probabilities) that the computer produces. To give a basic example, in an equation where factors besides age and amount of money donated are unchanging, the estimated coefficient of age might be 23 dollars, meaning that a person's likely donation goes up by that amount for every year older they get. We can come to a fairly reasonable decision about whether or not this $23 figure's coefficient actually equals zero with the help of the probability and t-statistic that a good piece of software will produce when it estimates the coefficient. The researcher can safely conclude that age has little predictive utility and mark it for exclusion from the prediction equation when the computer results indicate a high probability that its coefficient is zero.

METRIC DATA ANALYSIS

Analysis of Variance ANOVA

Quite frequently managers are concerned with knowing about differences over many groups or cases. An effective apparatus for these functions is an investigation of discrepancy. Two basic variations are possible, known as one-way and N-way analyses.

One-Way Analysis of Variance: This technique would be used when an individual performing a study wants to see how three or more averages differ, as would be the case with someone studying mean donation levels across five different cities. The ANOVA, or one-way analysis of variance, is the proper parametric test for this situation, and it is closely related to the previously-discussed test. This test compares the difference found between two means to the standard error of difference, an estimated expression of those means' random variance. The more general ANOVA method works in basically the same fashion. It will measure the variance among all of the selected means (the five cities, in this example) and compare it to a random variance measure (which in this situation would be the five cities' combined variances). To be specific, a significance probability and a test statistic can be found by dividing the variance of values between the different cities by their internal variances using an ANOVA method. This statistical method is the F-ratio of which the T-statistic is a special case. We repeat that a combination of a high F ratio and a low probability may mean that the variants from one city to another are attributable to more than chance.

Association

Either the manager or the researcher will be interested in potential associations between variables in a large number of cases, whether the variables relate individually or in groups. Associated variables can be used to predict different variables entirely. Researchers can safely confirm that a variable or variable set has a direct impact on another if there is already a decent theory to that effect in place - bearing in mind that association and causation are distinct concepts.

Ordinal Data: Spearman Rank-Order Correlation

Using the procedure for Spearman's rank-order correlation allows researchers to accurately compare two ranked variables, like the way that a hospital ranks staff expertise and friendliness. In order to discover if there is a correlation between one variable's high ranking and the lower or higher value of a different one, the rho coefficient of Spearman will be vital. Rho will have a positive sign in the event the two rankings are moving in the same direction. If the direction is opposite, a negative sign will accompany rho. Whatever the trend is, rho will not exceed the range from one to zero, and rankings that have a true correlation will be indicated by a high rho value - close to one.

Correlation of Pearson Product Moment

This strategy looks for an identical result as the Spearman analysis does, although its purpose is applied to interval and ratio-scaled variables. Pearson correlation coefficients are between 0 and 1, appear in positive and negative forms and are typically denoted by the letter "r." In addition to the Pearson r, many statistical analysis programs also give the researcher a probability of "r's" true value being zero.

The Pearsonian r2, which is the square of this, indicates the proportion of the first variance illuminated by the relationship.

METRIC DATA

Simple Correlations

Researchers can also use the Pearsonian correlation coefficient to analyze the r-value of a line plotted between points linking measurements on a graph: a low r indicates that the straight line makes a poor representation, while a high r value indicates that the line is well-suited to its task. See Figure 10.4 for examples of a well-fitted line (1) and one that fits poorly (2).

Multiple Regression

Once reliable predictive results are achieved using one variable to predict another, researchers can dig further to find out if the results can be improved by adding another variable or two. This is normally done with the tool multiple linear regression.

A metric variable which is dependent can often be predicted by combining different independent variables in a linear combination; multiple regression can build this combination in a way not too different from standard correlation of two variables. (When a regression equation variable is nominal - that is, it is set to one or zero to indicate whether or not a particular characteristic applies - it is called a dichotomous variable.) One example could be predicting the amount of tickets a baseball team sells per game given the month, day of the week, opposing team being played or weather.

A computer can help an uncertain researcher narrow down his or her selection of variables to consider for this kind of multiple regression in two different ways. In the first method, the researcher will pick out meaningful variables ahead of time according to a hypothesis that estimates which ones are most likely to yield useful, accurate predictions.

Researchers will be able to strike down predictors that are probably not significant after they get a look at the computer's initial t-statistic output, which shows the likelihood of any particular variable's coefficient actually equaling zero. That might have to be tried a few times before one can decide on the best predictor variable set.

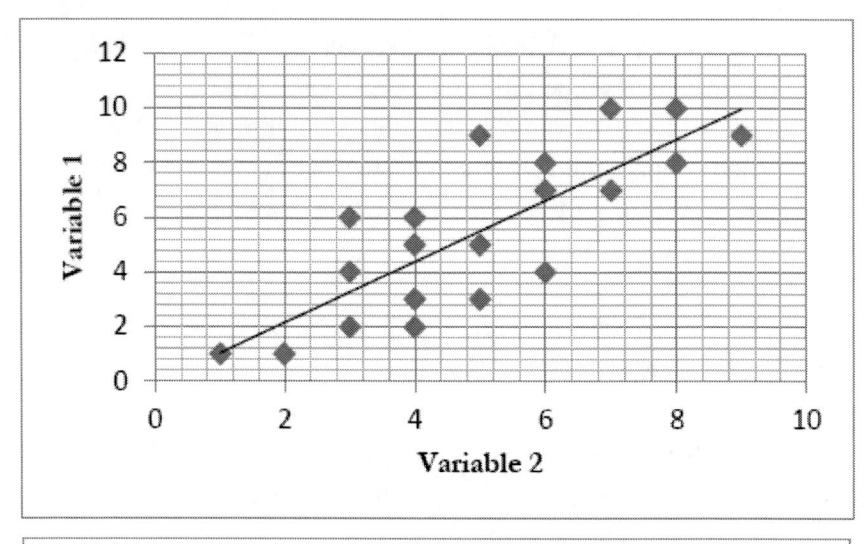

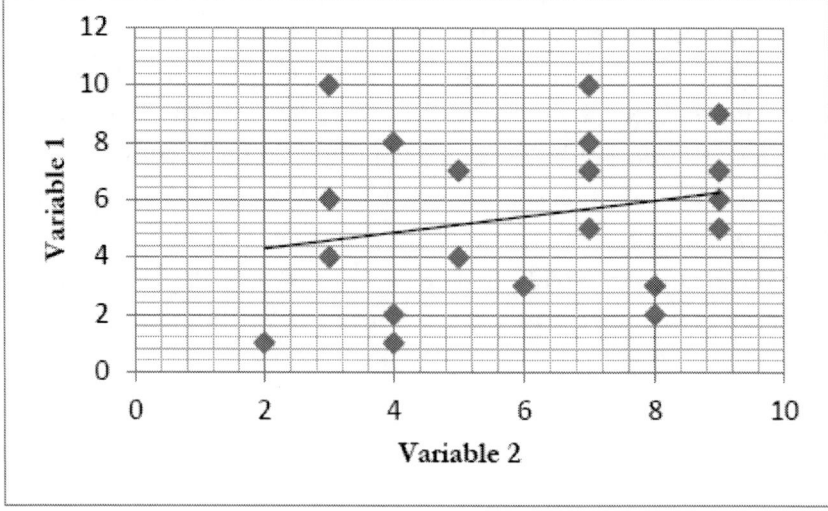

Figure 10.4. Variant Regression Lines.

Stepwise Regression

A procedure called stepwise regression analysis is used alternatively by the researcher using the computer to look for the best set of predictors.

> *When the study is at the exploratory phase, one good strategy is stepwise regression.*

The computer will start this procedure with the dependent variable's original variance; it next plugs a prediction factor into the equation, chosen for the maximum possible explanatory power. Subtracting out the variance explained by this variable, computing new correlations of each remaining potential predictor variable and the adjusted dependent variable, and then picking the variable with the highest correlation is what the computer does next. The candidate set's variables are incorporated into the equation for prediction this way until there are no more variables left or until a predefined point for stopping occurs, such as when the variance (see the next step) falls below 1 percent. When the study is at the exploratory phase, one good strategy is stepwise regression. Researchers always should be careful, though, because a meaningful predictor can be overlooked in this sort of analysis if the predictor correlates very highly to a variable that is included early on in the analytical process.

There are three measures that the researcher receives from the software that will be of interest when the multiple regression analysis is complete:

1. The Multiple R quantifies how adequate the equation matches the data. The probability of that statistic being actually zero is essential as an indicator that the equation actually does forecast.
2. The R2 multiple corresponds with the Pearsonian r2. What this shows is how much variation in the dependent variable can be explained with the linear combination of the predictive variables. The chances that the multiple R winds up equaling zero are no more important than this. When there is a large dataset, you may have a very significant multiple R to represent an equation

explaining a small amount regarding variances in the dependent variable.
3. Variable Coefficient Standardization - The role that each variable plays in the final prediction equation is something that the researcher will likely be very interested in discovering. It would be a mistake to try to compare the different sizes of the predictor coefficients' variables in order to discover this, since different variables usually use different units; the coefficient for sex, for instance, will be misleading since its value is binary and is usually 0 or 1, but the income coefficient will probably be quite modest since income values are normally expressed in dollar amounts in the four-to-five range. The answer to this problem is to do a conversion of the variables into units of standard deviation. These are called beta coefficients. They consist of the old regional coefficients, which can be called B coefficients, which are then divided by their respective standard deviations. Those variables that have a greater impact on the outcome of the prediction as a whole will have high beta coefficients, while the coefficients of less vital variables will be smaller.

OTHER MULTIVARIATE TECHNIQUES

There are, of course, more complex analysis methods to be considered by the researcher who already understands the basic techniques that were just described. The end of the book gives a list of sources that offer details on using other approaches.

Factor Analysis

Within a study many of the measurements may be related. If a study has a large database, it is frequently valuable to find out if the measurements obtained may be reduced into a smaller set of sub factors which relates to each set of measurements. The amount by which measurements correlate to each other can be determined through factor analysis, which also gives at least one factor derived from the information set. In addition, factor analysis takes into account every variable in a set all at once.

The huge field of indicators - ninety-two of them - was consolidated into a more reasonable five-factor set which still accurately represented local economic and social concerns by the Research Division using a piece of software designed for factor analysis:

- A factor of wealth and income
- A labor-structure and employment-field factor
- A factor representing the frequency of minority and poor counties
- A factor for population growth
- An age factor tracking both adults' ages and the presence of children in the household.

Cluster Analysis

The tendency of individual subjects to fall into tight groups with common characteristics is something that marketers are usually very interested in. Within the groups (as well as the heterogeneity across the groups), cluster analysis is designed to assist with this type of problem by taking whatever information the researcher has on each object and developing groupings that maximize the uniformity. First, there is clustering from the top down, where the researcher achieves the ratio of homogeneity-heterogeneity she is looking for by starting with an all-inclusive group of objects and dividing and subdividing it one step at a time. The program begins with each object in its own group and proceeds to combine them into groups until a specified stopping point is reached in bottom-up clustering.

Discriminant Analysis

In most correlation analyses, (both simple and multiple) dependent variables are measured metrically; there are certain cases, though, where marketers' interest is focused on a nominal measure. Along with regression, another technique that can produce variable sets that help users nominally categorize individual respondents into classes is discriminate analysis. Discriminate function is the equation that is the predictor of who belongs to a particular collection. When the researcher needs to draw a line between multiple groups, though, discriminate analysis quickly becomes complex, involving multiple functions. A second important difference is that discriminate analysis does not produce a statistic like R2 that indicates how well the function predicts. The frequency the final function accurately predicts an individual's group membership is how researchers usually measure viability.

Understanding how objects in a group are perceived in relationship to each other is something that marketers in multidimensional scaling are interested in. Multidimensional scaling is a strategy used for positioning things within a physical or perceptual space. There are three measures employed in this technique: the objective analysis of facts about an object (e.g., square footage, staff size, programs used); the subjective measurement of the object's nature (e.g., opinions on overall desirability, impressions of services offered, judgments on the staff's professionalism); and the subjective comparison by respondents of different objects to one another according to their (the respondents') own values. In each case the routine of computer analysis creates a map that relates these objects within geometric space.

A lot of choices made by consumers have to do with trading off between the features that various alternatives possess. Respondents are asked about their ideal object (such as their ideal youth center) by multidimensional scaling studies that use subjective input in the form of either object ratings or similarities judgments. For instance, a manager planning a YMCA would be able to examine the set of respondents whose idea of the perfect youth center matches closely with that presented by researcher, (the perfect base of support for them), or find groups of people who are wholly unsatisfied with the concepts offered by the study. The last mentioned would constitute a possible idea for a whole new kind of youth center experience.

The consumer's preference ranking alternatives will depend on the extent to which he or she is willing to trade, for example, poorer staff knowledge and a longer drive for lower prices. Conjoint analysis is one strategy that can be utilized to see what such sacrifices will mean. The objects of a conjoint study can include products, services, or other choices; the study will describe them through tracking different attributes played against one another. The values that respondents assign to each dimension relative to each other can be determined by applying a conjoint analysis routine to consumer rankings. This will reveal which collection of specified attributes garners the most enthusiasm from the entire field of study (even those sets of attributes that the study does not specifically mention) and help to identify the specific respondents who would be most interested in a particular set of attributes, whether proposed or already existing.

Multivariate Analysis of Variance MANOVA

Mentioned earlier, an ANOVA design is just one of the cases in which the person conducting the study is probably interested in discovering the points that differentiate groups with regards to particular metric characteristic sets.

Based on potential interest by a manager in a combination of outcomes, a researcher might want to examine the two manipulations and their effect on the average length of time customers spent in the store, the total sale amounts of high-priced merchandise, the sum of all poster sales and the portion of full price item sales as compared to discounted item sales. This kind of question can be answered with MANOVA, (multivariate analysis of variance) which operates in a fashion similar to ANOVA and produces similar results.

Chapter 11

MAKING IT COUNT

The prior chapters have provided an outline for planning and carrying out a functional and cost-effective research project and also have provided a vast array of strategies to help you do so. Now is the moment a manager or researcher has to jump in and figure out how to get everything done, which may be difficult if the budget is tight. The task of building systems is usually quite complicated. The researcher needs to list the basic requirements for carrying out a beginner's research program to see some of the ways in which it may be possible to keep costs down. Such requirements can be divided into three wide groupings: ideas, people, and things. Below is a partial list of the various requirements for each category. There are several tricks of the trade that researchers working on a tight budget can employ in each of the categories.

If the manager only has a small research budget and little research knowledge, what is the best way to make the most of it and add to it?

Now is the moment a manager or researcher has to jump in and figure out how to get everything done ...

Early in the book, an approach was outlined in which the knowledgeable and persuasive research manager could demonstrate the benefits that additional research expenditures could bring in an attempt to justify those expenditures; there are several sources of additional funding that should be explored. The research manager has to do this to tempt the manager who initially approved the research budget to add to it because he or she believes it will be valuable in the long run. An excellent place to start is to teach the manager in question about funding research based on this book's benefit-cost principles. Regardless of whether or not the stakes are low, it is important for managers to learn to distinguish how much information that has been gathered is actually useful for good decision-making.

GENERAL MISUNDERSTANDINGS OF RESEARCH

One issue might be that the superiors of the research manager are held back by the misunderstandings previously discussed. An implementation of a new way of thinking is crucial by the person in charge of the analysis to help eliminate concerns believed by those who govern him or her. Management also needs to become knowledgeable about the amount of affordable research options that this book outlines. But the researcher needs to always be looking out for chances to demonstrate just how research can help a specific problem.

If the manager only has a small research budget and little research knowledge, what is the best way to make the most of it and add to it?

It could be wise during the process to utilize an unauthorized research demo project that does not cost too much. There may be a time when the researcher knows there is the chance to show and not simply explain how research might be used to improve a specific management decision. When feasible, a smaller pilot study should be conducted by the researcher utilizing available funds. Even though this strategy has its risks, it is hoped that the ad hoc study results will turn out to be so intriguing that the manager will authorize a budget for the adventurous researcher after the work is done.

OTHER ORGANIZATION DIVISIONS

When the researcher has the good fortune to be working for a very large organization, such as a nation-wide non-profit organization with several branches, there may be other researchers in other divisions available to collaborate and help keep costs down. Doing projects together often enables more affordable and effective results than you would get from pursuing them individually. Research might not, however, be an initially enticing prospect to different divisions. If that is true, there are times when the researcher can find ways to suggest to other parts of the company how valuable this research has been. Later, financial contributions for projects could be petitioned for on a marginal cost basis. After a joint mission has succeeded, other parts of the company might be lured into the endeavor.

There could be projects where cooperation by the competition would be preferable to doing no research whatsoever, even if they will naturally share the results. For instance, a few small hardware stores might band together to do a survey about the effectiveness of doing cooperative advertising. If that kind of research project is executed, there should be a sharing between organizations of the expense as well as the process. As an alternative, you could set up a joint task force. This process will allow every participant to make a meaningful contribution to the final shape of the project; full participation from all contributors is more likely, even if the task force is vulnerable to project delays and conflicts. Privacy becomes an issue when funds for the project are acquired in this way.

Additional Partners

There may frequently be additional organizations with similar interests that could be convinced to partner with you in a research project. Even though there is mutuality, it is still possible that the competition could find out about the project if the partners do not agree to maintain confidentiality.

Universities or Wade Association

Collaborating with competitors on research in the private sector cannot only cause issues with confidentiality and conflicts of interest, it can even raise the ugly specter of antitrust violations. Moreover, cooperative projects can end or be compromised if disagreements arise over who is in charge, what is to be done, who works on which facet, and how the results will be utilized. It could be wise to use the services of a neutral person for help with such a project. There are a lot of obvious benefits, such as the savings that are inherent in a nonprofit's tax-free standing. To improve respondent participation and candor, consider having the project under the sponsorship of an association or university. In addition, a university will likely perceive research projects as a chance to advance scientific inquiry and academic careers, and they might be willing to help out financially.

A researcher and a staff that has been dedicated to the research project can carry out whatever tasks a year-long program requires. As an alternative, most everything could be taken care of by exterior agencies. Professional market research companies have specialized proprietary tools, like one-of-a-kind product-testing procedures, that they can employ in order to satisfy the research needs of a manager, no matter what they might be.

Sadly, no information exists to tell what functions are most frequently given to outsiders. Most organizations will not typically do their own field interviews because it would necessitate individuals who have been specially trained but who would only work in spurts as they are needed.

The majority of companies do not relish the idea of managing a considerable part-time labor force like that. Field research agencies hired from the outside may be able to achieve the results that individual companies might not. Since focus groups require unique interviewing skills to be effective, this function is often contracted out. It is likely, though, that a novice researcher with low budget will have little financial capability to employ a lot of external assistance. Thankfully, there are many additional and helpful low-cost or free sources that might be available to the researcher.

The Manager's Own Organization

A researcher working for a large enough company may get help from co-workers in a different analytical/report-preparing division. A few of the possibilities might be:

- *The Department of Long Range Planning:* There are economists and others who have a significant amount of social service education who can help when it comes to analyzing statistics.
- *QC Department:* There will be many people in this field who have a working knowledge of testing for significance and designing proper experiments.
- *Marketing and Advertising Departments:* Those who have just been hired with an M.B.A. and a concentration in marketing might very well have learned the latest methods and procedures for doing market research.
- *The IT and Accounting Departments:* Those areas of the organization frequently employ programming professionals or people who know how to handle large data sets.
- *Department of Public Relations:* Such specialists are frequently good at creating newsletters and could be helpful with design and graphics. These technicians also have extensive knowledge of computer programs for getting those graphics and designs printed.

- *The Word Processing and Secretarial Staff:* This department is where you can get helpful recommendations about word processing software. In addition, it could be where a researcher can find someone who can produce appealing surveys, do precise research reports, and prepare complex numerical tables.

Universities with graduate or undergraduate business programs can help in more than one way. A professor who does consulting could be hired for free or at least for less-than-market if he or she thinks there will be some valuable results coming out of this that could be used in the classroom. When looking for research help, a researcher should not limit his or her options only from students of business or economics programs. People studying psychology, public health, education, or social work can help if they have skills in designs, computers, or statistics. Additionally, they may impart good group dynamics skills and psychological insight to focus group leaders. For observation studies, an anthropologist might be desired.

Professors can have downsides too, and a researcher must be cognizant of these. If professors are not paid well, they might not be motivated to rush to meet the researcher's deadlines. At universities, students in the graduate programs are often looking for a 'side-hustle' to make some extra income. Graduate students are especially good at implementing roles rather than in designing them, particularly in spots where they are the ones technically trained, as with doing computer programming and statistical analysis. While this is a great opportunity, the researcher should remain watchful and cautious when engaging students, even when they are M.B.A. students. Even Ph.D. candidates cannot offer guidance on formulating problems and designing research if that requires a seasoned professional.

Nonprofit organizations may have possibilities for research assistance that other types of organizations can only get if they pay quite a bit for it. A resourceful nonprofit researcher could call upon the following sources:

- *Pro Bono Specialists:* A chosen number of professional industries support their members in donating their time to voluntary service in worthwhile activities.
- *Association Member Volunteers:* Knowledgeable corporate executives often volunteer to be on the boards of nonprofits they believe in. Although a few of these board memberships are geared more toward adding to the executive's resume or to facilitate business contacts with other members of the board, a large portion of board members may be diligent, helpful workers. It can be difficult for a nonprofit manager to see the advantages of having the head of a local multi-service marketing research agency sitting on the board of directors, especially if the head of the research agency is viewed as taking a valuable place that would be better given to someone more useful. However, these people can be quite helpful to the research endeavor. They can provide volunteer staff for certain tasks, access to computer equipment and software, opportunities for piggybacking research, they can also provide direct advice themselves, encourage or assign their own junior staffers to provide technical advice.
- *Retired Executives:* Many retired managers are enthusiastic about utilizing their talents to do work that is helpful to society. In America, there is a long history of the Service Corps of Retired Executives offering assistance that is government sponsored to small businesses and non-profits. Wise and experienced counselors for researchers, these individuals are considering different ways of researching management problems.
- *General Personnel:* There are times when they are needed under certain circumstances. It could be preferable for managers to employ outside people to do specific research jobs, particularly if those jobs need unusual skills.

There are a few other possibilities when you need to get additional assistance at low or no cost. Volunteers are one option. Although the groups most closely associate with volunteer workers are nonprofits, some for-profit organizations (e.g., hospitals) use them too. Such assistants are perfect for many of the research jobs covered in this book that require little training and few special skills, such as:

- Filling and addressing mail questionnaire envelopes, tracking returns by mail and handling follow-ups
- Delivering or handing out questionnaires for self-reporting
- Taking down simple data, such as the number of customers looking at a display, the number of cars parked at a competing store or recording and looking up the data on the license plates of cars parked at a mall
- Transcription of addresses from a guest book, expense-account voucher data or other archival records
- Finding relevant competitor's ads on social media, internet sites, magazines, local papers, etc. and taking screen shots or clipping/copying for reference
- Experimental assistance
- Basic analysis in situations where a computer cannot be used.

Volunteers can handle more complex tasks, like conducting interviews over the phone or in person, entering questionnaire data, processing data or conducting field experiments if they receive the proper training for such jobs. It is key to do training. Asking for voluntary participation can seem like the perfect way to keep costs down. Frequently, they are overeducated for the tasks you want to give them, and many of them will show commitment.

In contrast, volunteers can be costly in their own way. Volunteers frequently want autonomy and are not easily managed. The education, social status and motivation of many volunteers can be part of the difficulty. Several people think the organization should just be thankful they are helping, so they get rather patronizing. That frequently means they will show disdain for particular types of work. Those who think they can make more money somewhere else or who have more education than the researcher might argue in order to get things done differently. It is made perfectly clear to them what standards of performance are expected, and they are told that anyone not performing to the extent and at the quality level the research requires will be "fired," and this is why the researcher or manager should be careful about using volunteers unless they are carefully trained. Volunteers usually respond favorably to being treated as responsible professionals who have an obligation to their organization to do excellent work.

When researchers require a very specialized sort of academic rigor, advanced students make excellent people to hire. A student may also be a temporary worker who carries out many of the daily tasks that research studies necessitate. Five academic instruments exist for that:

- *Case Studies:* Business classes at universities frequently assign pupils the task of conducting an authentic example investigation as a major course task. Many students will already understand what they want to study, but there will be others who have not come to a final conclusion and can be influenced by a researcher's suggestions.
- *Work-Study Programs:* Some schools have students enrolled in work/study programs so that they only go to class part of the week and work the remainder of the time. A researcher on a tight budget would have to give a salary to work-study research aides, but these workers would have pretty low wages and would be more sophisticated and intellectual than the usual part-time person that could be hired.
- *Students in Independent Study Programs:* Many schools allow students to assemble their own independent study projects that will give them academic credit.
- *Internships:* Most Universities require an internship program in the discipline in which the student is studying. Some internships are paid, and others are not. These typically require the student to work in an organization for 10-15 hours per week and report back to the professor. This is great experiential learning for the student as they perform "on the ground" projects.

- *Volunteers from the community:* Many universities develop programs that involve students in community service.
- *Graduate School Dissertations:* Many researchers have found that candidates for master's degrees or doctorates can be excellent research assistants when they are offered the opportunity to contribute their academic research to the study in exchange for additional data and the professional experience available.

If the researcher on a budget likes this possibility, the first thing to do is contact the deans of area business schools to tell them of their interest in matching the needs of students and faculty with the needs of the organization and its research. A general overview of the types of projects in which the organization would be interested as well as a brief description should be included. Researchers who solicit some interest from the school itself will find themselves invited to make a personal visit or provide expanded information to present to students.

There are both advantages and disadvantages to utilizing students. One such advantage is the fact that they will be intrigued with the learning potential of the project. That means the researcher has to be ready to educate them about the organization and about the ways research is really done.

Another benefit is that most students are not hired by the organization. An organization can still do a lot to control what is being done, even by volunteers. When hiring students, both sides must have a clear understanding of the goals. It would be beneficial to have written agreement indicating the mission and timeframe.

Keep in mind that there are some disadvantages when utilizing students for the research project:

- Remember that a student will have additional responsibilities. This means they might not work as rapidly as the company needs them to and could miss significant appointments and deadlines.
- The tasks in a project will need to be fit into a semester schedule, unless they are graduate students working on an independent

Making It Count 183

study. That means students should not be taken on in order to make commitments to long term projects.
- Students, particularly those from Ivy League and elite schools, are occasionally arrogant. They will have learned from their professors what is the most current management, marketing, and technology ideology. Should the research not be conducted with this technology or not be enthusiastically embraced, a student might get patronizing or try to steer things in a different direction. A new researcher might think this is a problem if he or she lacks of self-efficacy on how to use the current research techniques. Conversely, the result is often that a researcher might find that the students are the best teachers.

Public libraries or government services are yet another possible resource. Governmental organizations from the local public library all the way up to the Department of Commerce, the Department of Agriculture, and the Bureau of Labor might assist the researcher in gathering background information and compiling secondary source data. Librarians can utilize Internet data retrieval systems to find the expertise that is needed to deal with such systems and could even agree to do affordable computerized searches for the new researcher.

Database research services are viable options as well. Researchers who do not get the help they need from a librarian can take advantage of the paid services of providers that specialize in doing secondary source analysis - for instance, gathering article citations on technological developments or competitors. There are also services that offer reproductions of the articles on the Internet for the researcher to use.

A researcher on a tight budget might be tempted to try to get the information from routinely contacted clients, but that really equates to employees becoming the field survey workers. Obviously, you can save money doing this, and you would expect that employees would have a pretty high response rate if they were going to interview clients they have selected. However, remember, having employees do the job this way can have many significant drawbacks:

- They may very well resent having to take on the assignment. That means they could rush the job and make big mistakes in either the commission or the omission.
- If they are allowed to choose their own participants, employees might very well select those who are easy to find or who will say positive things or at least no negative things about the staff person's own performance. That makes it more probable that they will choose their preferred customers or the ones they believe will provide the most positive answers.
- The employee may want to use the interview as an advertising opportunity. That will not only add bias the results of the moment, it may also ensure that you lose this customer for possible future research studies. The patron might be apprehensive and feel they are being deceived and will withhold information or will alter their replies, even if the personnel refrain from advocating anything.

A researcher on a tight budget might be tempted to try to get the information from routinely contacted clients, but that really equates to employees becoming the field survey workers.

The personnel department can help with employing and training part-time staff and evaluating those who are working in the research endeavor.

The purchasing department can be of assistance if the researcher wants to employ exterior suppliers to provide research services. Those in purchasing can find other suppliers, set procedures for bidding and rate the bidding submissions that come in. With the help of company attorneys, they can develop a contract with their supplier to make sure that the needs of the researcher are going to be met in a timely manner and as affordably as possible.

There are also several examples of research organizations that have reduced their overhead and addressed issues of non-responsiveness by setting up ongoing programs to maintain respondent pools full of agreeable subjects.

Piggybacking can be used effectively. This is when a researcher gets to add his or her questions to a survey designed by someone else, and it is something that both national and local surveyors allow. Marketing questions can be presented along with questions about other topic areas such as personnel and public relations, and this can even be done within a researcher's own organization. Such additional studies should be chosen with care to ensure that the basic topics will not influence the marketing results.

Some research suppliers perform studies where many different organizations use one omnibus instrument or series of them to pool their questions. Participants can split overhead costs with this method, but a drawback is that each researcher's questions are pooled with those made by others, introducing potential biases in the collected data.

Lastly, you can use exterior computer databases. There are a few organizations with databases of different types of market data. The organizations that supply and maintain this data can conduct secondary analyses on it according to the researcher's instructions, and some of them will also let the researcher purchase the raw data to do his or her own computerized analysis. One system that works in a similar manner is the PRIZM system.

Software Requirements

Anyone planning to pursue an ongoing research program needs to have the following types of software. These are listed in order of lessening importance:

- *Word Processing:* Software that does word processing is necessary to draft proposals, write questionnaires, create observation protocols, or code manuals and get final reports ready. For studies done by mail where label preparation and customized cover letters for each survey taker are needed, it is helpful to have a word processing software program with the ability to perform mail

- *Spreadsheet Software:* Microsoft Excel (or Numbers if using a MacOS) has spreadsheet software that is able to take down the research raw data and do some simple analysis. Input from spreadsheets can be entered into a majority of the available statistical software programs. In addition, appealing tables and graphs can be quickly generated and inserted into reports or presentations.
- *Statistical Software Package:* The price of a good suite of statistics software is a very sound investment for those organizations that know they will have ongoing research requirements. SAS and SPSS are the two industry leaders for full-featured software suites dedicated to statistics with the larger research agencies. They all come in PC versions also, but such systems are usually complicated and costly and take some time to learn. A new researcher might decide to begin with a simpler strategy. Minitab is one of the less costly statistical packages that include every major statistical procedure that we discussed in the chapter regarding statistics.
- *Graphics Software:* With powerful graphics, a report that is dull can be made more attractive and clear. A vast array of software packages for graphics can accomplish this. A majority will utilize the normal bar and pie charts, but a few will even create intense three-dimensional displays. Questionnaires and documentation can now be generated with complex, appealing headlines, graphics, charts, and figures in addition to ordinary text, tables, and graphs thanks to modern improvements in the capabilities of desktop publishing software. The very basic features offered by first-generation software for word processing and image manipulated have been far surpassed by their modern equivalents.
- *Additional Software:* Time and money might also be saved by the use of some other types of software available to the user. Websites

and programs now exist that assist in preparing questionnaires, create, and monitor samples, and assist and keep track of phone interviewers.

The smart researcher will take measures to familiarize him or herself with the strengths and weaknesses of the different software suites available before selecting one to buy, first by investigating review evaluations in independent journals and consulting with friends and colleagues. Next, be attentive to how software systems are compatible in style and the way materials such as data files, tables, graphs, and wording can be interchanged. The little irritations introduced by incompatible software and programs that do not work together are much less common with today's popular all-in-one systems such as Microsoft Office.

CLOSING THOUGHTS

The goal of this book was to earnestly try to provide a simple, logical, and cost-effective framework for the small to medium sized organization. Marketing research can be very intimidating for managers who have little to no experience in this area. The functional approach attempts to take what has traditionally been the scientific approach to research and turn it around.

Remember... to make no decision or to remain stagnate with your product offerings can be very costly in today's hyper-competitive environment.

By doing this, the nature of the problem becomes more manageable and easy to understand. Businesses cannot afford to undertake research projects for the mere sake of research alone. They are usually very purposeful with specific decisions and tasks that need to be legitimized and supported. Remember, to make no decision or to remain stagnate with your product offerings can be very costly in today's hyper-competitive environment.

On the Ground

Matt has just concluded his three month campaign. After segmenting his customers by zip code, household number of cars, and car type, he was able to build a promotion campaign, including mailers and posted advertising, to hold three themed events, one at each location. His three themes were:

- How to detail and clean a car properly.
- Fun day with Ford owners!
- Normal DIY maintenance for any car owner.

All three events were a huge success. He was able to leverage the knowledge of his employees, bundle themed based products increasing the average sale price by 27 percent. Also, he had a raffle onsite that collected valuable new customer data for him to use. He has now started working on his product delivery options and will continue with the events.

APPENDIX 1. ONLINE RESOURCES

@ResearchInfo.com - FREE Marketing Research Resources 21/4
www.researchinfo.com/

Online Marketing Resources | NC SBTDC
www.sbtdc.org/resources/online-marketing-resources/

Online Marketing Research & EFM Resources | MarketTools, Inc.
www.markettools.com/KnowledgeCenter

Market Research World
www.marketresearchworld.net/

Market Research Resources | One of the Leading Market Research
www.amplituderesearch.com/market-research-firm.shtml

Lightspeed Research - Online Market Research Resource Center
www.lightspeedresearch.com/resource-center/

Market Research Training | Online Training | Research Rockstar
www.researchrockstar.com/

Conducting Online Market Research: Tips and Tools | Inc.com
www.inc.com › Sales and Marketing › Marketing › Market Research

Marketing Research Plan: Tips for Online Marketing Research and ...
www.easy-marketing-strategies.com/marketing-research-plan.html

Market Research Resources | USDA FAS
www.fas.usda.gov/.../market_research/market_research_resources.asp

Online Panel and Market Research Resources | GMI | Global Market ...
www.gmi-mr.com/solutions/resources.php

Market Research and Entrepreneurship Resources
www.unk.edu/.../Market_Research_and_Entrepreneurship_Resources..

FREE Online Market Research Toolkit | Zoomerang
www.zoomerang.com/market-research/

MarketingProfs: Marketing Resources for Marketing Professionals
www.marketingprofs.com/

Sources for Market Research Information
www.Internetworldstats.com/sources.htm

Resources|Authentic Response
www.authenticresponse.com/market-research-resources

DIY Online Marketing Research
www.slideshare.net/ccplbusiness/diy-online-marketing-research

Survey Software, Online Surveys and Enterprise Feedback ...
www.vovici.com/

Appendix 1 191

Direct Marketing Research and Resources, Special Reports and ...
www.directmarketingiq.com/

Free Market Research To Help You Stay Competitive
www.marketing-strategies-guide.com/free-market-research.html

Conducting Market Research | Entrepreneur.com
www.entrepreneur.com/article/217388

A Complete Market Research, Online & Offline Marketing, Branding .
www.globalmarketingresources.com/

Market Research - Research Access - Resources for the Market ...
researchaccess.com/

Online Research
www.discoveryresearchgroup.com/online-market-research/

Market Research Services & Resources | MarketTools, Inc.
www.markettools.com › Market Research

Online Resources - Marketing Research - Research Guides at St ...
guides.stedwards.edu/marketingresearch

Online & Panel Research
www.synovate.com/research-services/online-panel-research/

Online Market Research
www.amplituderesearch.com/online-market-research.shtml

Online Marketing Research Analysis | Social Media Articles
socialmediahot.com/...marketing/online-marketing-research-analysis

SecondaryData.com - Marketing Research Online
www.secondarydata.com/marketingresearch/

Research Guide for Online Industry Market Research Planners by ...
www.bizminer.com/resources/guides/market-research-plan-data.php

Market Research Guide | Inc.com
www.inc.com/guides/marketing/24018.html

Online Marketing Research - Business.com
www.business.com › Sales and Marketing

International Marketing Resources ... - Online Marketing Degree
www.onlinemarketingdegree.net/resources/international-marketing-re...

→ Market Research Tutorial, Tips, and Training Resources | Power ...
www.powerdecisions.com/tutorials.shtml

Quantitative Market Research | Resource Nation | ResourceNation
www.resourcenation.com/.../quantitative-market-research-more-valua...

Online Market Research | Research Blogs
researchml.org/online-market-research/

Powerful Survey Tools for Better Internet Marketing Research
crowdscience.com/Internet_marketing_research_free

Industry Information
wnec.libguides.com/content.php?pid=33225&sid=243671

Are You Using These Free Online Tools to Conduct Market ...
frugalentrepreneur.com/.../harness-the-Internet-and-social-media-to-c...
5 Free Powerful Ways to Conduct Online Consumer Market ...

www.nichebot.com/blog/117/market-research/

Online market research sites for data, demographics and information
www.marketdirectionsmr.com/resources/resource-links/

Outsource online market research to Flatworld Solutions: online data
www.flatworldsolutions.com/research.../web-based-market-research-s...

Primary Market Research Sources
www.smsource.com/primary.htm

Secondary Market Research Resources - Entrepreneurship.org
www.entrepreneurship.org/.../resource.../secondary-market-research-...

Marketing research
www.jlrothassoc.com/resources.html

Home | Marketing Research Association
www.marketingresearch.org/

Ask the Internet: a primer on desktop market research - The Miller ...
www.millergroupmarketing.com/.../ask-the-Internet-a-primer-on-des...

GOVERNMENT

Government Market Research Reports
www.marketresearch.com › Home › Browse Research › Public Sector

Do Your Market Research | SBA.gov
www.sba.gov › ... › Starting a Business › Thinking About Starting

Export.gov - Market Research Index
export.gov/mrktresearch/

Market Research Analysts : Occupational Outlook Handbook : U.S. ...
www.bls.gov/ooh/Business-and.../Market-research-analysts.htm

Welcome to Market Connections
www.marketconnectionsinc.com/

Market Research, Industry Research - Wall Street Executive Library
www.executivelibrary.com/Research.asp

Government Data Resources - Market Research - Research Guides ...
libguides.rutgers.edu/content.php?pid=117971&sid=1017319

Government Resources » Free Market Research for Your Home ...
www.sparkplugging.com/government/free-market-research-for-your...

Demographics, Consumer Spending, Economy Data | Sponsored by ...
www.sbdcnet.org/industry-links/demographics-links

Conducting Market Research? Here are 5 Official Sources of Free ...
www.sba.gov/.../conducting-market-research-here-are-5-official-sour...

Market Research | USDA FAS
www.fas.usda.gov/agx/market_research/market_research.asp

www.census.gov

SEGMENTATION

Market Segmentation (Business Reference Services, Library of ...
www.loc.gov › Researchers

Market Segmentation
www.businessplans.org/segment.html

Appendix 1

5 Market Segmentation - Examstutor.com - an a level and
www.examstutor.com/.../resources/.../marketing/market.../5_market_...

Best Practices | Market Segmentation
www.pointclear.com/solutions/market-segmentation.php

Market Segmentation - GeoLytics
www.geolytics.com/resources/market-segmentation.html

Market segmentation | Marketing and sales | Library | ICAEW
www.icaew.com/en/library/subject.../marketing.../market-segmentatio...

Market Segmentation - Customer Segmentation - Psychographic ...
marketsegmentation.com/

Market Segmentation | KnowledgeBrief
www.kbmanage.com › Business Concepts

Market Segmentation | Industry Research – Amárach Research
www.amarach.com/resources.htm

Specializing in customer market segmentation research and ...
www.franklynn.com/resources/?c=182514

Secondary Data Sources
www.allnetresearch.com

www.bitpipe.com

Secondary Data Sources - American Marketing Association
www.marketingpower.com/Community/.../Research/SecondaryData

www.markektingtools.com

www.lexis-nexis.com

Primary and Secondary Data Sources
www.scribd.com/doc/7179744/Primary-and-Secondary-Data-Sources

Secondary Data Sources - Marketing Research for PhD Students ...
guides.library.uwm.edu/content.php?pid=29285&sid=214949

Secondary Data Analysis
www.hd.gov/HDdotGov/detail.jsp?ContentID=352

www.marketresearch.com

SecondaryData.com - Home
www.secondarydata.com/

www.dowjones.com

www.profound.com

www.usadata.com

These information based URL's change frequently, however, the root URL should be consistent.

MARKET RESEARCH INTELLIGENCE

American Marketing Association (AMA)

Alliance of International Market Research Institutes (AIMRI)

Advertising Research Foundation

Appendix 1 197

Council of American Survey Research Organizations (CASRO)

European Society for Opinion and Market Research (ESOMAR)
Focus Vision

Greenbook

Marketresearch.com

Market Research Association (MRA)

PMRG

Quirks

Research and Markets

SCIP

HSMAI Hospitality Market Research Firms

Yahoo Market Research Directory of Market Research Firms

Top 25 Market Research firms

MRS

Emarketer

APPENDIX 2. SAMPLE SURVEYS

SAMPLE SURVEY 1

1. Please indicate if you agree or disagree with the following statements:

	Strongly Disagree	Disagree	Undecided	Agree	Strongly Agree
Product is affordable	○	○	○	○	○
Product is valuable	○	○	○	○	○
Product is better than other products on the market	○	○	○	○	○
Product is easy to use	○	○	○	○	○

2. How likely are you to recommend [Product/Service] to a friend or coworker?

○ 1 – Will not recommend
○ 2
○ 3
○ 4
○ 5
○ 6
○ 7
○ 8
○ 9
○ 10 – I will recommend

Appendix 2

3. How satisfied are you with this [Product/Service]?

   ○ Very Dissatisfied
   ○ Dissatisfied
   ○ Neutral
   ○ Satisfied
   ○ Very Satisfied

---

4. What would make you more satisfied with this [Product/Service]?

   [   ]

---

5. Compared to our competition, do you feel [product/service] is

   ○ Less expensive
   ○ Priced about the same
   ○ More expensive
   ○ Not sure

---

6. Do you feel our current price is merited by our product/service?

   ○ Yes, the price is about right
   ○ No, the price is too low for your product
   ○ No, the price is too high for your product

---

7. What is the…

Most amount you would ever pay for a product like ours? [   ]

The least amount you would feel comfortable paying? [   ]

Appendix 2 201

SAMPLE SURVEY 2

1. How long have you been a customer?

   [   ]

2. In the past month, how many times have you used our product?

3. How satisfied are you with our product? Please use a 5-point scale, where 5 is Extremely Satisfied and 1 is Not Satisfied

   ○ 5   ○ 4   ○ 3   ○ 2   ○ 1

4. Please rate the following attributes using a 5 (best) to 1 (worst) scale

	5	4	3	2	1
Price	○	○	○	○	○
Durability	○	○	○	○	○
Color Selection	○	○	○	○	○
Ease of Use	○	○	○	○	○

5. Compared to our competition, where do we rank?

   ○ 1st
   ○ 2nd
   ○ 3rd
   ○ 4th-9th
   ○ 10th +

6. What can we do to make this product better?

7. What is your gender?

○ Male
○ Female

8. Please select your age

○ Less than 18
○ 18 to 24
○ 25 to 34
○ 35 to 54
○ 55+

SAMPLE SURVEY 3

1. We're planning an event for Halloween. Which date is best for you?

   [ ]

2. Would you prefer the event was in the morning, afternoon or evening?

   ○ Morning
   ○ Afternoon
   ○ Evening

3. We have a few ideas for location. Where would you want this event to take place?

   [ ]

4. Do you have any theme ideas for the party?

   [ ]

5. What activities do you think you would enjoy?

   1. [ ]
   2. [ ]
   3. [ ]
   4. [ ]
   5. [ ]

6. What are your five favorite foods?

1.

2.

3.

4.

5.

SAMPLE SURVEY 4

1. How did you hear about this event?

   [   ]

2. How do you rate this event location?

   ○ Poor
   ○ Below Average
   ○ Average
   ○ Good
   ○ Excellent

3. How do you rate the content that was presented?

   ○ Poor
   ○ Below Average
   ○ Average
   ○ Good
   ○ Excellent

4. Would you be interested in volunteering at our next event?

   ○ Yes
   ○ No

5. Please list any other comments or suggestions about the event.

   [   ]

Sample Survey 5

Please take our quick survey to assess your satisfaction with [Product X]. We look forward to reviewing your responses. Thank you for your time and feedback!

---

1. Please rate your overall satisfaction with [Product X]. Please use a 5-point scale where 1 is Very Dissatisfied and 5 is Very Satisfied.

   ○ Very Dissatisfied
   ○ Dissatisfied
   ○ Neutral
   ○ Satisfied
   ○ Very Satisfied

---

2. Please rate [Product X] on a 5-point scale where 1 is Poor and 5 is Great

	Poor 1	2	3	4	Great 5
Quality of the product	○	○	○	○	○
Length of life of product	○	○	○	○	○
Design of the product	○	○	○	○	○
Consistency of quality	○	○	○	○	○

---

3. Please rate the delivery of [Product X] on a 5-point scale where 1 is Poor and 5 is Great

	Poor 1	2	3	4	Great 5
Speed of delivery	○	○	○	○	○
Quality of delivery	○	○	○	○	○

---

4. Please rate the staff for [Product X] on a 5-point scale where 1 is Poor and 5 is Great

	Poor 1	2	3	4	Great 5
Courtesy from staff	○	○	○	○	○
Representative's availability	○	○	○	○	○
Representative's knowledge	○	○	○	○	○
Complaint resolution	○	○	○	○	○
After sales service	○	○	○	○	○
Technical service	○	○	○	○	○

5. Is there anything that [Product X] could have done to improve your satisfaction?

Sample Survey 6

Thank you for taking our customer service questionnaire.

It will only take 2-3 minutes to complete. We appreciate your business and value your opinion. We'll use your opinions to take stock of our service and support, and to make improvements.

---

1. How did you last contact customer service?

   ○ Website contact form
   ○ Email
   ○ Telephone
   ○ Other (please specify) _____

---

2. If you have a customer service issue number or representative's name, please enter it here.

   [   ]

---

3. General satisfaction

	Very Dissatisfied	Dissatisfied	Neutral	Satisfied	Very Satisfied
Overall, how happy are you with our customer service?	○	○	○	○	○
Overall, how satisfied are you with our products?	○	○	○	○	○

Appendix 2

4. How satisfied are you with our customer service representatives related to the following aspects

	Very Dissatisfied	Dissatisfied	Neutral	Satisfied	Very Satisfied
Promptness	○	○	○	○	○
Courteous	○	○	○	○	○
Helpful	○	○	○	○	○
Knowledgeable	○	○	○	○	○
Efficient	○	○	○	○	○
Understood my needs	○	○	○	○	○

5. Where do we need to improve the most?

- ○ Response time
- ○ Wait/Hold time
- ○ Friendliness
- ○ Courtesy
- ○ Knowledge
- ○ Ability to listen
- ○ Patience

6. Compared to our competitors, would you rate our customer service as

- ○ Better
- ○ Same
- ○ Worse
- ○ N/A

7. From a customer service perspective, would you recommend us?

○ Yes   ○ No

8. What else could we do better? Do you have any other comments?

9. Please add your email address and full name if you would like us to follow up with you

Name

Email

SAMPLE SURVEY 7

1. In the past week, how many [Product X] advertisements have you seen?

   ○ 0
   ○ 1
   ○ 2
   ○ 3
   ○ 4 or more

2. Where have you seen advertisements for [Product X]?

   ○ Newspaper/Magazine
   ○ Social Media
   ○ TV
   ○ Internet
   ○ Other (please specify)

   [ ]

3. What stuck out to you the most about the ads for [Product X]? What do you like or dislike about them?

   [ ]

4. Please choose how much you agree or disagree with the following statements about [Product X].

	Strongly Disagree	Disagree	Neutral	Agree	Strongly Agree
Advertisements are interesting	○	○	○	○	○
Claims in advertisements are believable	○	○	○	○	○
Advertisements clearly show what is being offered	○	○	○	○	○
I plan to buy [Product X] in the future	○	○	○	○	○

Sample Survey 8

1. How satisfied are you?

	Very Dissatisfied	Dissatisfied	Neutral	Satisfied	Very Satisfied
With your job?	○	○	○	○	○
With your direct supervisor?	○	○	○	○	○
With the team spirit in your work environment?	○	○	○	○	○
With your morale?	○	○	○	○	○
With your overall job security?	○	○	○	○	○
With the company as a place to work?	○	○	○	○	○

2. How much do you agree with the following:

	Strongly Disagree	Disagree	Neutral	Agree	Strongly Agree
I am optimistic about the future of the company.	○	○	○	○	○
I am proud to work for the company	○	○	○	○	○
I feel that the company cares about its people.	○	○	○	○	○
Men and women are provided with equal career.	○	○	○	○	○
I understand the company's strategy.	○	○	○	○	○
The company is a leader in the industry.	○	○	○	○	○

APPENDIX 3.
TOP GLOBAL MARKETING RESEARCH FIRMS

Australia
- OzTAM
- Roy Morgan Research

Canada
- Léger Marketing
- Print Measurement Bureau

France
- Ipsos

Germany
- GfK
- Psyma Group

India
- IMRB International
- RNB Research

Netherlands
- Segment Y

Russia
- Bazis IG

United Kingdom
- Datamonitor
- Dunnhumby
- Euromonitor International
- Illuminas
- Ipsos MORI
- Kantar Group
- Mintel
- Research International
- Synovate
- Taylor Nelson Sofres (part of the Kantar Group)
- YouGov

United States
- Arbitron
- BCC Research
- C.A. Walker Research Solutions
- Decision Analyst
- Forrester Research
- Gartner Group
- Hall & Partners
- Harris Interactive
- Illuminas
- IBISWorld
- International Data Corporation
- IMS Health
- J. D. Power and Associates
- Kelton Research

- Leo J. Shapiro & Associates
- Medimix International
- NPD Group
- Nielsen
- O'Donnell & Associates
- Off Madison Ave
- Rockbridge Associates, Inc.
- SIS International Research
- StrategyOne
- SymphonyIRI Group

Turkey
- Eksen Research

ABOUT THE AUTHORS

David Smith, D.B.A., M.B.A., C.M.C., professor of management and marketing at Palm Beach Atlantic University and a former management consultant with Arthur Andersen, has worked with the Department of Commerce, Small Business Administration, Foreign Agricultural Service, Export Development Corporation and numerous economic trade and development groups. Included in his consulting experience has also been work with numerous Fortune 500 firms seeking market expansion, export capital acquisition, and enhanced global operations and logistics. Having over 30 years of international experience, he has forged valuable contacts throughout the world often speaking at national and international conferences on the topics of Strategic Management, Marketing and International Business. Lastly, he is also a noted researcher, with over 50 completed industry research projects, academic peer reviewed publications and presentations.

Barbara VanderWerf, M.B.A., is a professor at Palm Beach Atlantic University, currently teaching management and leadership. With over a decade of experience in higher education, Ms. VanderWerf is considered an expert in the classroom, developing innovative approaches to curriculum delivery. Her area of management experience is in the area of organizational efficiencies, culture, and leadership. As the principal consultant at E2 Management Consultants, her focus is on small and medium sized firms seeking to become leaner and more profitable. Her background also includes time at a Fortune 500 firm. Her current research interest is in current higher education management as it relates to management theories and practices.

INDEX

A

archives, 58, 67, 68, 89
arithmetic mean, 153

B

B coefficients, 168
biases, 64, 76, 85, 86, 90, 107, 137, 138, 185
bimodal, 154

C

central tendency, xi, 148, 152, 153, 154
Chi square test, 159
cluster analysis, 169
competitors, 5, 6, 25, 26, 28, 59, 66, 74, 86, 124, 126, 129, 130, 176, 183, 209
computer software, 148, 154
conjoint analysis, 171
convenience experimentation, 108
convenience sampling, 107, 108
cost of uncertainty, 45
cross-tabulations, 160

D

data entry errors, 133
databases, 9, 63, 66, 68, 92, 185
debriefing, 75, 85
decision framework, 24, 46
decision rules, 44
decision theory, 42, 43, 45
degrees of freedom, 160
depth interviewing, 144
descriptive information, 26
descriptive statistics, 148, 149
discriminant analysis, 170

E

experimental designs, 83
experimentation, 17, 79, 80, 81, 83, 89, 122, 123
explanatory information, 26, 27

F

F ratio, 163

Facebook, 118, 122, 124, 125, 127, 129, 130
face-to-face interviewing, 106
factor analysis, 168, 169
focus group rooms, 104
focus groups, 53, 101, 102, 103, 104, 109, 121, 122, 127, 130, 135, 177
free market, 191, 194

G

graphic scales, 143
graphics software, 186

I

insights, 59, 73, 97, 111, 120, 121, 123, 125, 126, 130
instagram, 118, 122, 129
interval data, 151, 161
interviewer-induced error, 136
IT (information technology) center, 63

L

level of significance, 158
librarians, 183
Likert scales, 142
low-cost sampling, 101

M

mail studies, 92
mall intercepts, 105, 107
marketing research program, 14, 15
mean, 74, 85, 93, 112, 134, 144, 148, 149, 150, 154, 155, 156, 158, 162, 163, 171
measures of dispersion, 155
metric data, 154, 155, 163, 165
Microsoft Excel, 186

Minitab, 186
modal value, 153
multidimensional scaling, 170
multivariate analysis of variance, 171
multivariate analysis of variance (MANOVA), 171
multivariate techniques, 168

N

network sampling, 111
nominal data, 149, 155, 159, 160

O

observations, 9, 67, 74, 76, 78
one-way analysis of variance, 163
ordinal data, 150, 151, 155, 164

P

Pearson correlation coefficient, 164
perceptual map, 6
physical traces, 75, 77
predictive information, 27
prototype report, 51

Q

qualitative research, 109, 149
questionnaire design, 101
quota sampling, 107

R

random digit dialing approach, 99
ratio data, 151, 152
Request for Proposal (RFP), 31, 39
respondents, 90, 98, 112, 134, 170

S

sales reports, 59
screening, 111
secondary sources, 64, 65
semantic differential, 142, 143
social media platforms, 97, 117, 122, 124, 126, 129
social media research, 123, 128, 130
spreadsheet software, 186
standard deviation, 155, 156, 157, 168
standard error, 148, 156, 161, 163
Stapel scale, 143
statistical analysis, xi, 49, 51, 149, 150, 152, 155, 157, 158, 164, 178
statistical software, 186
statistical testing, 148, 161
survey designs, 101
survey research, 197
systematic observation, 74

T

telephone interviewing, 98
test marketing, 80
Thurstone scales, 142
Twitter, 118, 122, 126, 129

V

validity, 84, 136, 139